AUTISM
CAUSES
Prevention
and
Treatment

AUTISM

Vitamin D Deficiency and the Explosive
Rise of Autism Spectrum Disorder

CAUSES

Prevention

and

Treatment

NEW
TREATMENT
PROTOCOLS
FOR YOUR
CHILD

JOHN J. CANNELL M.D.

SUNRISE
River Press

SUNRISE
River Press

Sunrise River Press
39966 Grand Avenue
North Branch, MN 55056
Phone: 651-277-1400 or 800-895-4585
Fax: 651-277-1203
www.sunriseriverpress.com

Edit: Mary Van Beusekom
Layout and Cover Design: Connie DeFlorin

ISBN 978-1-934716-46-5
Item No. SRP646

Library of Congress Cataloging-in-Publication Data
Cannell, John Jacob.
Autism Causes, Prevention and Treatment / by John J. Cannell, MD.
    pages cm
Includes bibliographical references and index.
ISBN 978-1-934716-46-5
1. Autism in children–Diet therapy. 2. Vitamin D–Therapeutic use. I. Title.
RJ506.A9C36 2013
618.92'85882–dc23

                                                          2012045793

Printed in USA
10 9 8 7 6 5 4 3 2 1

DEDICATION

This book is dedicated to Professor John McGrath and his research group at the Queensland Brain Institute in Australia. It was by reading their work that I concluded that vitamin D is intricately involved in autism. In 2001, McGrath and his research group first concluded, "Thus, chronic vitamin D deficiency should be examined in more detail as a candidate risk factor for neurodevelopmental and neurodegenerative disorders."[1] Autism is the classic neurodevelopmental disorder.

CONTENTS

Foreword

by William Grant, PhD

A s many as 1 in 68 eight-year-olds in the United States has autism.[1] The lifetime cost of autism per person with autism in the United States and the United Kingdom—estimated at $2.4 million—is staggering.[2] Because the incidence is rising rapidly, we must identify the cause of the rapid rise and how to reverse the trend and improve the lives of those with autism. This book synthesizes a wealth of information on the evidence that low vitamin D concentrations are an important risk factor for autism. The book is written in a style accessible to parents with autistic children, yet it has more than 300 references to peer-reviewed journal publications so physicians and researchers can review the evidence.

ORIGINS OF THE VITAMIN D THEORY OF AUTISM

The idea that low maternal concentrations of the active form of vitamin D are a risk factor for problems in fetal brain development was first proposed by John McGrath in papers on schizophrenia[3] and on various adult disorders.[4] Later, his group was able to demonstrate that vitamin D deficiency during pregnancy negatively affected fetal brain development.[5] John Cannell, MD, originated the theory that high doses of vitamin D reduce the risk of autism and are useful in its treatment.

He began to study the literature in 2001 and founded the Vitamin D Council in 2003 to present the information on the health benefits of vitamin D to the public.

In 2004, Cannell began considering whether vitamin D deficiency could explain the rapidly rising autism epidemic. Two years later, he published a paper on influenza, "Epidemic Influenza and Vitamin D,"[6] in the journal *Epidemiology and Infection,* presenting his theory that influenza is seasonal due to seasonal variations in ultraviolet B (UVB) sunlight availability and vitamin D production. This theory has been supported by randomized controlled trials (considered the gold standard of studies) in the United States and Japan. He published another paper, "Autism and Vitamin D,"[7] in the journal *Medical Hypotheses* in 2008. According to Google Scholar, as of July 2014, this paper had been cited 146 times, including many citations in papers supporting or expanding aspects of his theory.

The key aspects of his theory are:

- Vitamin D has important roles in brain development.
- Vitamin D reduces inflammation, which is associated with autism.
- People born in less sunny regions or with darker skin have elevated rates of autism.
- Treating patients with the bone-softening disease rickets (associated with vitamin D deficiency) with high doses of vitamin D apparently reduces the occurrence and severity of several autistic symptoms.
- People with Williams syndrome, who generally have higher concentrations of the active form of vitamin D, usually have characteristics opposite those of people with autism.
- The rapid rise of autism during the past 20–30 years coincides with medical advice to avoid the sun and wear sunscreen when in the sun.

Research findings since publication of Cannell's papers have strengthened the evidence that UVB light from the sun and vitamin D concentrations affect the risk of autism. In support of his theory, a study in Denmark found that vitamin D concentrations in the adult population dropped from 26 ng/mL (nanograms per milliliter) in 1993–1994 to 21 ng/mL in 1999–2001 to 18 ng/mL in 2006–2008.[8] Reinforcing this finding, a study found that autism prevalence by state for children 6–17 in the United States varied by more than a factor of two between states with the highest and lowest UVB availability in October for both whites and blacks; it also found that blacks had about a 25 percent higher prevalence of autism than whites.[9] However, the study was unable to determine whether autism developed in the uterus or in the first few years of life.

SO WHY ISN'T VITAMIN D WIDELY ACCEPTED AND PROMOTED?

In 2012, healthcare in the United States cost, on average, $8,233 per person, and it accounted for 18 percent of the gross domestic product. To keep up revenue and profits, the healthcare system does what it can to discourage competition from alternative approaches. Physicians who try to incorporate practices outside the accepted practice guidelines find that insurance companies won't pay for the practices. The profit-oriented healthcare system appears to view vitamin D as strong competition to business as usual because it has been shown to effectively reduce the risk of many chronic and infectious diseases and is very inexpensive.

One way the healthcare system has tried to marginalize vitamin D is by treating it as if it were a pharmaceutical drug and by requiring expensive and time-consuming randomized controlled trials before it will accept that it can be used to prevent and treat many types of disease. That might be OK if properly designed and conducted randomized controlled trials had been performed; however, very few trials demonstrating the link between vitamin D deficiency and disease have been reported. Unfortunately, many trials were not terribly useful because they used only 400–1,000 units per day of vitamin D_3, did not measure vitamin D blood concentrations, enrolled people with reasonably high vitamin D concentrations, and showed no understanding of the expected vitamin D concentration–health outcome relationship.

Although a few vitamin D randomized controlled trials were properly conducted and had positive outcomes, they tended to be for minor rather than major health outcomes. But that is changing. Today, six major vitamin D trials are under way with expected completion dates of 2018–2020. The next major review of vitamin D will likely occur in 2020.

Vitamin D is not a pharmaceutical drug but rather a molecule manufactured in the body or obtained through diet or supplements, or both. As such, it should be judged by the criteria appropriate for evidence-based nutrition. These criteria were proposed by A. Bradford Hill in 1965 in a talk before the Royal Society of Medicine in London.[10] The primary criteria for drawing conclusions about vitamin D include strength of association measurement, consistent findings in different populations, relationship between dose and response, plausibility, evidence (e.g., from a randomized controlled trial), agreement with other findings, and ruling out factors other than vitamin D that could otherwise be responsible for the results. These criteria have been largely satisfied for vitamin D for such health outcomes as breast and colorectal cancer, cardiovascular disease, dental caries, all-cause mortality, multiple sclerosis, and acute respiratory infections.

In addition, when the vitamin D–health outcome relationships for these diseases are examined, they all look similar: they show a rapid reduction in negative health outcomes for small increases of vitamin D above the lowest values (about 5–10 ng/mL), then progressively slower reductions until values of 30–40 ng/mL or higher are reached. The point of this discussion is to suggest that, while Dr. Cannell has proposed an impressive theory of how vitamin D deficiency may explain much of the autism epidemic, it seems unlikely that the US healthcare system will accept it anytime soon. Although some experts may admit that vitamin D does have merit for preventing and treating autism, doing so might be considered akin to letting the camel get its nose under the tent, opening the door to more widespread acceptance of vitamin D.

A Credible Theory

John Cannell is a very committed man, one who will stick with a project for a decade or more until he is satisfied with the outcome. He also focuses on one narrow topic at a time, which is an attribute of "broad autism phenotype," a set of characteristics he learned he had two years ago. His personal understanding of autism, specialty in psychiatry, and deep interest in vitamin D make him ideally suited to study the role of vitamin D in autism. Thus, readers should consider implementing Dr. Cannell's recommendations under the supervision of a physician willing to accept the possible role of vitamin D in autism to ensure that the proper vitamin D concentrations are reached.

Dr. Grant is a former NASA physicist and is now one of the most prolific vitamin D researchers in the world. He has made numerous important discoveries about the relationship between sunshine and various health conditions. His organization, the Sunlight, Nutrition, and Health Research Center, is on the Web at www.sunarc.org.

PREFACE

This book makes the case that vitamin D is useful in preventing autism and that high doses of vitamin D are useful in treating some people with autism spectrum disorder (ASD). As this book goes to press, several groundbreaking studies about vitamin D and autism have just been published or submitted for publication. One study, by Rhonda Patrick and Bruce Ames,[1] involved searching genetic databases. They discovered that activated vitamin D directly regulates at least six proteins that are abnormal in ASD. They also discovered the answer to the serotonin paradox, which is the long-known fact that autistic people tend to have high levels of serotonin in their blood but low serotonin levels in their brain. Patrick and Ames discovered that activated vitamin D regulates both enzymes that make serotonin but regulates the enzymes in different directions.

Vitamin D decreases production of blood serotonin enzyme but increases production of brain serotonin enzyme. So when you are low in vitamin D, the blood enzyme can't turn off serotonin production, and your blood levels rise. However, those same low vitamin D levels mean there is not enough serotonin brain enzyme, so your brain serotonin level is low.

Patrick and Ames also confirmed what I have written about estrogen-salvaging vitamin D enzymes by making the enzymes more efficient, so fewer girls have autism than boys. They also showed that one mechanism of autoimmunity in ASD has to do with serotonin that the body has already processed.

Another study, by Eva Kočovská and colleagues from the Neuropsychiatry Centre, Institute of Neuroscience and Physiology, Sahlgrenska Academy, University of Gothenburg, Sweden,[2] is the first family study of autism and vitamin D. Family studies are important because they allow you to compare an autistic person's vitamin D levels with the levels of his siblings and parents—not just a community control group— and get an idea if the differences may be genetic.

The authors chose the Faroe Islands to do their study for several reasons. The islands are located in the north Atlantic at latitude 62 degrees north, which means a prolonged vitamin D winter (the number of months that the sun is too low on the horizon for adequate sunshine to penetrate the atmosphere and make vitamin D in the skin). The Faroe Islands also have a maritime climate (high rainfall and strong winds), with an average summer temperature of only 48 degrees F. This means that people in the Faroe Islands wear a lot of clothes and make less vitamin D than people in warm, sunny climates. However, the Faroe Islanders have a diet rich in oily fish (which contain vitamin D), which means that they probably get most of their vitamin D from their diet. These two factors increase the chance that any differences in vitamin D levels between the ASD group and their families may be due to genetics.

Kočovská et al. measured vitamin D levels in 40 autistic people ages 15–24. They found that their average vitamin D level was about half that of their siblings and parents. This study may simply mean that autistic people stay inside more often or eat a different diet (less fish) than their siblings or parents. Another possibility is that, somehow, the ASD process lowers vitamin D levels. However, in my opinion, the most likely cause of their findings is that the inherited vitamin D metabolic machinery (or "system") of ASD individuals is different than that of their typically developing peers.

A third study, by Khalid Saad and colleagues,[3] compared the vitamin D blood levels of 122 Egyptian children with ASD (ages 3–9) to 100 typically developing children. The median vitamin D level of typically developing children was twice that of autistic individuals. They also found that vitamin D blood levels directly correlate with the severity of the autism (the lower the vitamin D levels, the worse the autism). Of the ASD group, 106 subjects had low vitamin D levels and were given 5,000 IU/day of vitamin D_3 for three months. Eighty-three of the 106 completed three months of daily vitamin D treatment. Collectively, 80 percent (67/83) had a significantly improved outcome on autism rating scales, mainly in items testing problematic behavior, eye contact, and attention span.

This is the first study suggesting that high-dose vitamin D helps in the treatment of autism. It is an open-label (early) trial, which does not carry the weight of a randomized controlled trial, so definitive proof is still lacking. However, the response rate was 80 percent (80 percent of the 106 ASD children improved with high-dose vitamin D), which is higher than the 30 percent placebo response rate usually seen in clinical trials of medication in people with ASD.[4]

This book explains hundreds of studies, all involving the link between vitamin D and ASD. Virtually all of the studies are directly relevant to the prevention or treatment of ASD. If you know anyone with ASD, have them or their caregivers read this book. However, please know that my recommendations about vitamin D supplementation and sunlight don't work for all children. In my experience, about 25 percent of children respond dramatically, about 50 percent respond significantly and 25 percent don't respond at all. Will it help your child? With at least 75 percent of children responding dramatically or significantly, the odds are in your favor, but the only way to know is to try it.

INTRODUCTION

AUTISM: FIRST IMPRESSIONS TO CURRENT THEORY

When I entered the exam room, the six-year-old boy was flapping his hand about six inches in front of his face. He seemed to not notice my presence—even though I was sitting directly in front of him.

I had just begun my third-year psychiatry rotation when my professor invited me to witness a "rare case." He told me only that the boy's referring physician had given him a diagnosis of schizophrenia, a mental illness characterized by disordered thinking and poor emotional responses. He advised me to observe the child without talking loudly or touching him. "You may only see one case like this in your career," he said. "If you don't properly examine and diagnose him, you may miss that case." If only that were so.

The mother said that her son developed normally until he was 15 months old, when he seemed to retreat from the world. Within a month, he lost spontaneous speech, forgot the 30 words he had learned, and avoided eye contact. He became clumsy, had trouble sleeping, and obsessively spun the wheels on his toys. When the mother told him it was time to sleep or eat, he responded by parroting, or repeating her words, and usually doing what she asked. He seemed happiest when alone. But when his highly regimented routines were disrupted, he flew into rages that lasted for hours.

When he was younger, he played with imaginary friends but no longer engaged in creative or imaginary play. If his mother changed the order of books on his shelf, he changed them back. The boy ignored kids his age when they visited his home. During recess, he played alone, repetitively sliding down a slide—but only when no one else was using it. He seemed unaware of his parents' activities and had no friends in preschool. In fact, the school had recommended a special placement with children with developmental delays for the next year. When he was outdoors, he seemed to be in a world of his own, deep in thought, not noticing the people with him or the sights and sounds around him. The boy read obsessively about several seemingly unrelated subjects but particularly loved books about wheels and spinning. He had chronic, severe constipation with occasional large, hard stools. Laxatives helped but caused diarrhea, which upset him.

The mother had taken her son to his pediatrician after his problems began but was told that he would outgrow them. Since then, in a desperate search for answers, they had seen a neurologist, psychiatrist, psychologist, and two other pediatricians. None could agree on a diagnosis or suggest treatments. The mother said that mental illness didn't run in her family, although her husband, an accountant, was quite introverted and had no friends. He had sent a 22-page letter describing his son's problems.

I left the exam room no more enlightened than when I went in. My professor looked disappointed when I agreed with the diagnosis of schizophrenia. "No," he said, shaking his head. "He has autism." It was 1975—long before autism became an everyday word. Years later, I learned that I, too, had a mild form of the same condition (see sidebar "When My Research Became Personal" on page 7).

Fast forward to my graduation from medical school. I opened a primary care clinic in West Virginia. Within a few years, the clinic was caring for thousands of families within a 25-mile radius. I didn't see a single patient with autism during the 1980s, despite medical staff at my clinic caring for and vaccinating an entire community of children. It seemed that my professor was right: autism was extremely rare. However, that changed after I completed a psychiatry residency in 1991 and started a practice in Montana.

Instead of seeing just the one child with autism my professor had predicted, I saw more and more kids who would not look at me. Many had never developed or had lost their language, "melted down" when they didn't get their way, and had few or no friends. Some concerned parents appeared remote but did not seem to have autism. This seemed to rule out a genetic cause or parental neglect. Although I didn't know it then, I was confronting the beginning of the autism epidemic—and physicians were as baffled as parents.

Today, 1 in 68 US children has autism. The rate for boys is five times higher than that for girls.[1] Those were the alarming statistics reported by the Centers for Disease Control and Prevention (CDC) in March 2014.[2] Even more disturbing was that the data were taken from a 2010 survey, suggesting that the figures were already outdated and, considering the trend, possibly even higher. How much have the numbers increased? How many of these autistic children will get better? What will become of them when their parents die or are unable to care for them?

Each year for the past 20 years, the number of children with autism spectrum disorder has increased 12 percent. The autism epidemic is a tragedy on a scale that is unlike any the Western world has faced in modern times. Families with autistic children are under enormous stress. They pay $20,000–$100,000 per year for care of their child; lifetime costs may total more than $3 million.[3] The divorce rate for families with an autistic child is double that for families without one.[4,5] In fact, a study shows that having an autistic child causes more stress than having one with a fatal illness.[6]

The billion-dollar question, then, is "What causes autism?" Why has it reached epidemic proportions? Is it preventable, treatable, or both? Theories and blame abound. Some parents point to vaccinations, despite scientific evidence otherwise. Another theory fingers a toxin developed and used starting in the 1980s, when the epidemic began, but scientists haven't been able to isolate it. Some scientists believe autism is a genetic disease but can't explain how a genetic disease could explode in one generation. Plus, 15 years of genetic studies have failed to identify such a gene or genes.

As a psychiatrist, I referred families with a child with autism for specialized care and learned as much as possible about the disorder. Meanwhile, I became interested in nutrition after learning that I had a vitamin B_{12} deficiency. Perhaps surprisingly, most physicians, including me, learned little or nothing about nutrition in medical school. But it was vitamin D that held my interest. In 1973, I spent the summer in Iran to learn to diagnose and treat rickets, a bone-softening disorder caused, in most cases, by vitamin D deficiency.

Vitamin D occurs naturally in only a few foods, namely fatty fish such as salmon and sardines. Infants get vitamin D through supplementation or consumption of vitamin D–enriched foods such as milk and formula. Interestingly, breast milk, the "perfect food," has no significant vitamin D. The only other natural way to get enough vitamin D is through exposure to the ultraviolet B (UVB) spectrum in sunlight, which prompts the body to produce its own vitamin D.

In 2001 and for the next 10 years, I read every available scientific paper and book on vitamin D. I was convinced that vitamin D could change modern medicine. Why? Because activated vitamin D is a steroid hormone (a molecule that is made from cholesterol and works via a dramatic mechanism of action; steroids turn genes on and off) crucial to good health, and most of us don't get enough of it. Since the 1980s, when the autism epidemic began, well-intentioned doctors have told us to avoid the sun or use sunscreen to prevent skin cancer—with unintended consequences. Properly applied sunscreen can reduce our bodies' production of vitamin D, so we need to either consume foods containing vitamin D or take supplements to avoid a deficiency. However, until recently, doctors didn't suggest taking vitamin D supplements to compensate for lack of exposure to sunlight.

I began to write scientific papers about vitamin D in 2003, after I was convinced that vitamin D was intimately involved in influenza epidemics. That same year, I founded the nonprofit Vitamin D Council, a group that educates people about the dangers of vitamin D deficiency. Finally, in 2004, at a shopping mall, I had an epiphany. I noticed that toddlers and even some infants were drinking fruit juice—not vitamin D–enriched formula or cow's milk—from their bottles and sippy cups. In the 1990s, cow's milk, which has been fortified with vitamin D for 50 years, became suspect due to its links to protein allergies (food allergies caused by a particular protein found in a particular food) and lactose intolerance, an inability to digest the sugar lactose in dairy products. I knew from the literature that few parents gave their toddlers vitamin D supplements despite the American Academy of Pediatrics' recommendation.

I also noticed that most white children had pale skin in midsummer. Perhaps this was because vigilant parents followed pediatricians' recommendations to use sunscreen or protective clothing while their children were in the sun. Or it could be the result of parents keeping their children indoors because, due to the social deterioration of neighborhoods, they feared for their children's safety. Or it could come down to kids' growing TV, computer, and video game use. Where then, I wondered, were these toddlers getting vitamin D? Developing brains have a strong need for vitamin D. Children who don't drink milk or eat fatty fish (not favored by many kids) don't have a good source of vitamin D after they are weaned from formula. Interestingly, weaning often happens shortly before some children first show signs of autism and get their first vaccinations.

After my moment of clarity, I was very eager to research autism and its link with vitamin D. How many autism facts could this vitamin D theory explain? Were there any autism facts that the vitamin D theory could not explain? I researched autism carefully and, in 2007, published a scientific article, "Autism and Vitamin D."[7]

In 2009, Emily Deans, MD, published an article on the theory in *Psychology Today*.[8] In 2010, an article in *Scientific American* asked, "What if vitamin D deficiency is a cause of autism?"[9] That same year, five Harvard University geneticists expanded on the vitamin D theory of autism, saying that vitamin D enhances the immune system and protects the genome from mutations.[10] Two years later, autism researchers led by Christopher Gillberg, MD, of Sweden's Gillberg Neuropsychiatric Institute, published a review of autism and vitamin D calling for urgent research into their relationship.[11]

Even more important, in 2012, researchers studied 50 autistic children, ages 5–12, during the summer, comparing them to 30 healthy children.[12] They found that the autistic children had much lower vitamin D levels than the healthy children, despite both groups having equal sun exposure and no vitamin D supplementation. Second, the researchers found that the lower the vitamin D level, the more severe the autism. This is why parents who let their autistic children outside in their bathing suits in summer usually report that the children are better in August than in February. Furthermore, the researchers' findings strongly suggested a vitamin D treatment effect.

Finally, the researchers found that 70 percent of autistic children had antibodies (proteins produced by the body's immune system when it detects antigens, harmful substances that can lead to illness) that were damaging their brain tissue; the lower the vitamin D level, the higher the number of antibodies. In addition, these antibodies were more numerous in children with severe autism than in those with mild autism. The authors concluded that their results "lend support to the hypothesis that autism is a vitamin D deficiency disorder."

In this book, I discuss autism and vitamin D and how proper (and safe) doses of vitamin D may: (1) prevent or lessen the risk of having an autistic child, if taken during pregnancy and by both parents before conception; and (2) improve (not cure) autism symptoms in autistic children and adults. If you are a parent of a child with autism, you are far from alone. I hope to share all I've learned over the years and help your family not just cope with autism—but thrive.

◆

WHEN MY RESEARCH BECAME PERSONAL

I never quite fit in; now I know why.

I am a physician and a researcher. I also have what is called broad autism phenotype. Rather than a diagnosis, broad autism phenotype is a set of observable traits similar to those in someone with autism spectrum disorder. People like me are usually uncomfortable in social situations, have poor emotional and facial recognition (ability to remember faces by mentally comparing them to a "face library" of people you've met before), tend to be reclusive, have few friends, and flounder in long-term relationships.

We are intensely interested in one narrow subject at a time, have rigid personalities, prefer to have everything in its place, are detail-oriented, can be ritualistic and repetitive, and do not like change.[1] My father, the late poet Skipwith Cannell, had similar traits—not surprising given the genetic component of broad autism phenotype.

I had been studying autism for many years when, only a couple of years ago, a physician confirmed that I had broad autism phenotype. A phenotype is the set of all one's observable traits. I was 64, and finding out was a relief because it explained so much about my personality and view of the world—and why I never quite fit in. It explained my painful shyness, social awkwardness, and long-term obsession with narrow or obscure subjects.

My social anxiety, or discomfort in social situations, and struggle to maintain long-term relationships, have tended to confuse and isolate me. My inability to remember faces limits my social interaction in that, if I go to a party, I end up introducing myself repeatedly to the same person. People, I've learned, do not like that. I am in behavioral therapy to help get me "out of my shell" and become more at ease with other people.

Autism traits that helped me improve education, health and healthcare

Some traits of broad autism phenotype, such as being detail-oriented and highly focused, have been very useful to me in my professional career. For example, after founding the Cannell Clinic in Flat Top, West Virginia, in 1983, I noticed that all of my coal-mining patients smoked cigarettes. To try to get them to stop, I launched a unique and controversial anti-smoking campaign that was featured in an article in *The New York Times*.[2]

Then came my 10-year obsession with education and teachers who cheat on standardized elementary achievement tests for recognition, prestige and, sometimes, cash bonuses. It led to exposure of this practice on large media outlets such as *60 Minutes*.[3]

I next turned my attention to false memory syndrome for another 10 years. False memory syndrome was a much-discussed subject in psychiatry in the 1990s. A depressed patient would see a psychiatrist for help managing the illness, and the psychiatrist would attribute the depression to parental childhood sexual abuse that the victim had blocked from memory. Some patients, who had no way of proving or disproving the theory, made public accusations that ended up destroying their family.

I helped end false memory syndrome by setting the stage for lawsuits against recovered memory therapists.[4] Hundreds of lawsuits emerged, many with multimillion-dollar verdicts. The result? Insurance companies stopped insuring therapists who did recovered memory therapy. And that was the end of a discredited—and, in many cases, devastating—practice.

How I take care of myself

I take 10,000 IU of vitamin D each day (The National Institutes of Health recommend a range of daily doses, from 400 IU for babies to 800 IU for people 71 and older[5]). IU is the unit of measurement for some vitamins. Because I have broad autism phenotype (which is genetic, or passed down from my parents, rather than acquired due to a vitamin D deficiency), the effects of vitamin D on my symptoms are modest. However, I do notice better facial recognition and less social anxiety.

I am fortunate in that I live in Southern California, so lack of sunlight isn't the problem it is in colder climates. I spend about 15–30 minutes per day in the sun when I have time, but I wear sunblock on my face and hands. Sunblock is a type of physical sunscreen that contains ingredients, such as zinc oxide or titanium oxide, to block ultraviolet radiation. This is because the face and hands get enough sun exposure over a lifetime. I don't like the chemicals in sunscreen (a chemical-based lotion, spray, or gel applied to the skin to absorb or reflect some of the sun's ultraviolet radiation), but sunblock with zinc oxide paste is like wearing liquid clothes.

My struggles and triumphs with broad autism phenotype have given me a deep empathy for people with autism spectrum disorder and their families. That's why it has held my rapt attention for so many years. Finding a cure for this condition is so important because it would spare our children—now and into the future—the isolation and frustration that people like me have endured our entire lives.

———————————

Chapter One

Reaching the Child Inside

Autism is a condition that is as hard to miss as it is to identify. Parents of autistic children often say, "I know he is in there, but it's like a switch is turned off. If I could only turn on a switch somewhere, he'd come back to us." This notion—that a "normal" child is inside your autistic child but unreachable—is both common and heartbreaking. Because there's no cure, the diagnosis is a life-altering event. In fact, depending on its severity, it can turn lives upside down.

Autism is a *spectrum disorder,* meaning that symptoms range from mild to severe and often overlap.

For example, a child with mild autism spectrum disorder (ASD) may have Asperger's syndrome, and a child on the severe end of the spectrum may have full-blown autism or childhood disintegrative disorder. People with Asperger's are able to communicate, if awkwardly, with others. However, they may be rigid, obsessed with narrow topics, and have difficulty "fitting in" socially.

A child with childhood disintegrative disorder, on the other hand, may meet initial developmental milestones, such as walking, but then deteriorates, no longer able to speak or communicate with others.

CHILDREN WITH "FASCINATING PECULIARITIES"

It may seem as if autism first emerged in the 1980s or 1990s, but it was actually first described in 1943. Physician Leo Kanner, writing in a premier medical journal of the day, reported on 11 children with strikingly odd behavior: "Since 1938, there have come to our attention a number of children whose condition differs so markedly and uniquely from anything reported so far that each case merits—and I hope will eventually receive—a detailed consideration of its fascinating peculiarities."[1] The children, he wrote, did not interact emotionally with others, became extremely upset by any break in routine, were fascinated by objects, and either used language strangely or not at all.

Kanner also noted lack of facial expression, poor eye contact, unusual vocal noises, and little use of gesture to substitute for speech. Many of the children, he said, were clumsy and did not meet the usual developmental milestones for rolling over, sitting up, standing, or walking. They made odd, repetitive movements (now called stimming), recoiled to touch, never engaged in imaginative or creative play, had temper tantrums, and had trouble imitating others—all while being seemingly oblivious to how their behavior affected others. Finally, he described children who were perfectly OK with eating dirt from the ground but refused most foods from the dining table.

Kanner himself implied that this behavior might indicate a new syndrome simply because he had never seen such children. He was 40 years old at the time and had been practicing psychiatry for more than a decade.

A year after Kanner's work was published, Hans Asperger described a group of dysfunctional children who could usually talk and often spoke like adults, although they sometimes rambled on.[2,3] He noted many of the same characteristics Kanner did, although some of the children had extraordinary abilities in math and memory.

Both Asperger and Kanner finally concluded that the syndrome was not new, just overlooked; however, the children they described, if they had lived in the 1920s, would have been hard to miss. Regardless, it was clear that, in the 1930s and 1940s, the disorder was extremely rare.

OUTSIDE LOOKING IN

Although its "official" symptoms are described in the *Diagnostic and Statistical Manual of Mental Disorders (DSM)* (the "bible" for mental health professionals), most people just sense there is something odd about children with autism. It is almost as if they are not in the room with you. They don't seem to look at you. (In fact, they do look at you, but only as part of periodic, rapid environmental scans.) If you touch them, many attempt to brush you off or block you. No matter how many children are present, autistic children often occupy themselves with their own solitary games or rituals; they may play for hours spinning the same object. If they speak, they often sound like a robot.

> Because the different types of ASD can overlap considerably and there's no blood or imaging test for it, diagnosis can be elusive.

Because the different types of ASD can overlap considerably and there's no blood or imaging test for it, diagnosis can be elusive. Professionals use two "official" *DSM-5* criteria to diagnose ASD: persistent deficits in social communication and social interaction with restricted repetitive patterns of behavior, interests, or activities.

- *Social Interaction:* Children with ASD have impaired social interactions characterized by awkwardness, blank facial expressions, restricted use of body language, and aloofness. The child usually has few, if any, friends and seldom has friends his own age. Most kids with ASD don't seem to share enjoyment, interests, or achievements with other people and do not react appropriately to emotional expressions.

- *Social Communication:* Communication deficits run the gamut from a complete lack of spoken language to the use of peculiar phrases and robotic or hard-to-understand speech (a condition known as apraxia of speech).

- *Repetitive Interests and Activities:* Children with ASD can flap their hand in front of their face, spin objects, or focus on a narrow part of an object for hours. Inflexible and easily disturbed by departures from routine, they may have meltdowns completely out of proportion to the change in routine. These tantrums can test parents' patience very quickly. For this reason, physicians often place self-destructive or violent autistic children on antipsychotic medications such as risperidone (Risperdal).

SYMPTOMS OF A WHOLE-BODY DISEASE

Some ASD children also have symptoms of a generalized disease, not just a brain disease. Some can withstand great pain. More than 35 percent have heartburn, and 60 percent have constipation.[4] Most have evidence of systemic inflammation and make antibodies to their own brain, so autism is itself an autoimmune disorder. Most boys with autism have a thin bone cortex. (The cortex is the outside, straw-like part of the bone that is evidence of bone growth).[5] Parents report that infections are common. Infections cause inflammation, which may damage developing brains.[6]

WERE DOCTORS PREVIOUSLY OBLIVIOUS TO AUTISM?

Some experts, mostly geneticists, still claim that the current wave of autism is entirely illusionary.[7] That is, they claim it is due to changes in diagnostic criteria that either now define well children as ill or imply that autism has always occurred at this rate. I have practiced medicine for almost 40 years, and the idea that doctors, teachers, and parents missed the symptoms of autism in the 1950s, 1960s, and 1970s strikes me as ludicrous. Unless they are mild, autism symptoms are hard to miss in the examination room, classroom, or living room. This better-diagnosis argument assumes that, for many decades, doctors, teachers, and parents were completely oblivious to one of the most obvious disorders in psychiatry and neurology.

Furthermore, autism treatment centers are common now, but in the 1970s, they were almost unknown, which indicates that the market is responding to a need. I doubt very much that any parent would take a well child for expensive treatment just because a doctor said their child was autistic. If the child is doing OK at school and home, it's extremely unlikely that parents would spend tens or hundreds of thousands of dollars on unneeded, time-consuming psychological treatments (the only ones that seem to lead to long-term improvement).

Another explanation is that the large number of autism cases is the result of "diagnostic drift"—that is, diagnoses have changed (drifted)—and that children who would have received a different diagnosis 30 years ago are now being diagnosed with autism.[8] However, psychiatric diagnoses were rare in children in the 1960s and 1970s, if for no other reason than child psychiatrists were rare as well. Certainly, no one recorded a childhood epidemic during that time of the kind or magnitude that could have drifted into autism over the years.

Experts who support the concept of diagnostic drift say that children born in the 1960s who would have been diagnosed with mental retardation, childhood schizophrenia, or obsessive-compulsive disorder (OCD), an anxiety disorder characterized by invasive thoughts, are now diagnosed with autism. Because of revised *DSM* criteria and ongoing research, some say diagnoses are drifting. This argument invites many questions. For example, the *DSM* added Asperger's in 1994. Does that mean it didn't exist before then? That it was ignored or lumped into another category? Or that it had become so common that psychiatrists could no longer ignore the diagnosis?

Diagnostic drift does not explain why so many parents are now desperate enough to seek expensive autism treatment. Also, mental retardation, childhood schizophrenia, and OCD are different from ASD in very important ways—particularly in speech and interpersonal communication. I agree that diagnostic drift accounts for some—but not all—of the increase.[9] And I'm afraid that the new *DSM-5* criteria may limit treatment access to some children who clearly need it.

Does Autism Have Genetic Components?

Some geneticists (although they are becoming rare) consider autism a classic genetic disease—the product of a genetic mutation (error) or mutations. But a classic genetic disease is unlikely to increase unless the people who have it reproduce much faster than others and pass

> If autism were a classic genetic disease, the diagnosis should be decreasing, not increasing.

the disease to their children. Autistic individuals seldom have long-term relationships, so they are unlikely to reproduce and pass on their genes. So if autism were a classic genetic disease, the diagnosis should be decreasing, not increasing.[10]

In fact, what I saw in my psychiatric practice in the 1990s was the opposite: I saw children with severe autistic symptoms but normal parents, grandparents, great-grandparents, aunts, and uncles.

However, the children sometimes had a brother or sister with autism, so it was a childhood epidemic—a new one. I also saw symptoms so severe that parents and teachers could not possibly have missed them—regardless of the decade.

◆

"REFRIGERATOR MOTHERS"

For many years, psychiatrists added guilt, shame, and stress to an autism diagnosis by blaming parents—especially mothers. Moms of kids with illnesses such as psychosis and autism were accused of being cold, "refrigerator" mothers. Today, few, if any, people believe that poor mothering causes these conditions.

TREATMENT: PHYSICAL AND MENTAL HEALTH

To date, the medical treatment for autism is only for recurring behaviors, not for core symptoms. Some randomized controlled trials show that both multivitamins[11] and fish oil[12] produce minor improvements in behavior. New antipsychotic drugs, such as risperidone (Risperdal) and aripiprazole (Abilify), reduce aggression and improve symptoms such as sleep problems.[13] Selective serotonin reuptake inhibitor antidepressants, such as fluoxetine (Prozac), may help improve mood and reduce violent behavior, while stimulants such as the amphetamine dextroamphetamine mixed salts (Adderall) may address attention-deficit symptoms.

Behavioral treatment can be quite effective but often takes several hours of therapy per week.

THE MOST COMPELLING REASON TO SEARCH FOR TREATMENT

Although not a criterion for the diagnosis, and certainly not a universal symptom, some autistic children are miserable. Parents are forever bound to their children's happiness, and most parents find it impossible to be happy when their child is miserable. Parents of autistic children can tell if their child is unhappy. Not all autistic children are chronically unhappy, but many are, and such misery is one of the hardest situations for parents to bear.

CHAPTER TWO

MANY CAUSES—OR JUST ONE? EIGHT THEORIES

For the past two decades, researchers, celebrities, and parents have promoted dozens of theories about the autism epidemic. Perhaps out of sheer desperation, people around the globe have constructed elaborate theories ranging from genetics and vaccines to conspiracies to poisons in the environment. I don't subscribe to these popular beliefs. Rather, I'm convinced that most ASD is caused by

a. immune system damage due to maternal or toddler vitamin D deficiency,
b. combined with an antigen (a noxious triggering event), and
c. in children with abnormal vitamin D genetics.

But no review would be complete without examining all major theories before I detail my own. So first let's examine eight theories based on genetics, damaged genes, vaccines, uncontrolled inflammation, autoimmune disease, mitochondrial disease, environmental toxins, and serotonin.

THEORY 1: AUTISM IS A GENETIC DISORDER

ASD has a genetic basis, but it's unclear how genes cause the disease.

One study suggested that, of a group of identical twins with autism, about 40 percent inherited it from their parents; for the other 60 percent, their autism likely was due to shared environmental factors (e.g., vitamin D deficiency, lack of exposure to the sun).[1] Siblings of those with ASD are about 10 times more likely than the general population to have some symptoms of autism. However, the genetic mutations—the damaged genes that should cause ASD—still have not been identified despite hundreds of millions of dollars of research.

Unlike Down syndrome, a genetic condition that leads to developmental problems, ASD cannot be traced to an abnormality on a single chromosome (the group of DNA "instructions" for the body).

ASD has a genetic basis, but it's unclear how genes cause the disease.

In addition, no genetic syndrome associated with ASD has been shown to always cause the disease. For example, only about 30 percent of children with the genetic disease fragile X syndrome, which is associated with ASD, actually develop ASD.

Before proceeding with this genetic discussion, the two words you need to know are genotype and phenotype. Genotype is what your *genes* are like (i.e., your entire set of genetic "instructions"), and phenotype is what *you* are like (i.e., tall or short, depressive or not, attached or detached earlobes). Genotype is supposed to dictate phenotype, but sometimes it does not. For example, if each cell in a person's body has three copies of chromosome 21 instead of the usual two, you could reasonably expect that person to have the characteristic phenotype of Down syndrome (e.g., slanted eyes, short stature, wide hands and feet, developmental problems). However, there are rare—and unexplained—exceptions to this expectation.

Also, researchers have been able to identify only a tiny number of

abnormal genes in which a genotype *always* results in the ASD phenotype. The best that scientists have been able to do is to detect de novo,
or new, point mutations (small duplications or missing information)
in the genotype of about half the kids with ASD.[2] To make it even more
complicated, few autistic children (or their parents) have these tiny
mutations in the same places on their DNA. How can that be if these
point mutations are the cause?

Nevertheless, genetic abnormalities such as fragile X syndrome
have been associated with ASD, but associations—even genetic ones—
do not mean they're the cause. That is, if A and B are associated, they
are associated in one of three ways:

- A caused B
- B caused A
- An unknown factor, C, caused both A and B

Throughout the history of medicine, some of the biggest mistakes have been made by scientists who ignored this association
principle.

So we have a disease with genetic characteristics: if your identical twin is severely affected, you have a higher chance of being autistic
(although the autism could range from mild to severe). But we also
have 20 years of fruitless searching for a common genetic cause. Could
we be looking in the wrong place? Few older relatives (e.g., parents,
grandparents) of autistic children have ASD, so clearly the disease is not
classically genetic. That is, it is not usually inherited by a parent who
then passes down a mutated gene to a child.

I have watched with despair as the autism epidemic increases on
continent after continent. I have seen ASD diagnoses skyrocket,
autism treatment centers spring up to meet rising demand, and the
number of disabled children multiply. Almost everyone knows of
at least one family affected by autism. But genetic diseases passed

from parent to child do not increase so dramatically in just one generation. The incidence of Down syndrome, for instance, has not changed for decades, so how could the condition have a genetic component (as in the case of twins)?

Before fully explaining the connection, let's look at the theory that damaged genes cause ASD.

◆

MISTAKES WERE MADE: BERIBERI, PELLAGRA AND BIRTH DEFECTS

Throughout history, scientists have had difficulty thinking outside the box or, in the case of ASD, thinking that the *lack of something good*, such as vitamin D, could contribute to a disease. Instead, they typically look for something bad, such as a malformed gene, toxin, or infection.

For example, Nobel Prize–winning Dutch physician Christian Eijkman discovered in the 1930s that milling rice to remove its outer shell caused the disease beriberi, a devastating and deadly illness we now know is caused by a lack of vitamin B_1 (thiamine) in the diet. Eijkman interpreted his findings to mean that rice contained harmful bacteria, and he theorized that the outer shell contained a natural antidote, or a medicine that counteracts the effects of a toxin. He thought that eating milled rice without the protection provided by the shell exposed one to the bacteria. He couldn't conceive that a lack of a good thing alone—in this case, thiamine, the B vitamin found in the husk—could cause beriberi. This is a perfect example of how physicians, even Nobel Prize winners, often blame a bad thing rather than a lack of a good thing.

A similar tale can be told about pellagra, a disfiguring and mentally devastating disease that killed a hundred thousand poor Americans in the South at the beginning of the twentieth century, when we started to mechanically mill corn, removing the niacin-rich shell. The niacin (vitamin B_3) content of corn-based products plummeted, pellagra soared, and people died. For decades, the medical profession thought a toxin in corn caused the disease.

They could not fathom that the absence of something good—niacin in the outer shell of the corn—could produce such catastrophe. Incredibly, 80 years after the discovery of the connection between niacin and pellagra, organized medicine finally gave up its infection theory and blessed the addition of adequate amounts of niacin to grain-based products, which cured pellagra. No wonder German physicist Max Planck said, "Science progresses one funeral at a time."

History tells another tale about birth defects and folic acid, a form of vitamin B_9. Women without enough folic acid in their diets often give birth to babies with birth defects that result in malformations of the spine (e.g., spina bifida), skull, and brain. Some babies have even been born with no brain at all.

Again, many in the medical profession failed to recognize the cause of the problem. Some even fought the solution: adding folic acid to grain products and prenatal vitamins.

THEORY 2: GENETIC INJURY CAUSES AUTISM

Another theory about autism involves genetic injuries, or genetic damage due to things in the natural environment, such as radiation, radon (naturally occurring gas that can cause lung cancer), and X-rays from the cosmos that are constantly passing through the body; toxins; and the products of combustion from consuming food. Scientists have identified numerous

> The important thing to remember is that the damage in these new, tiny mutations is not passed down from parent to child.

genes that appear to have been damaged in children with ASD, but only a tiny number of autism cases are attributed to these apparently damaged genes because they are on different places in the genome in different autistic children.

The large number of autistic individuals with unaffected family members suggests that the disease is associated with (not caused by) spontaneous tiny mutations in genes. Such mutations are common in almost everyone and can wreak havoc unless your body's DNA repair and maintenance system is fully functional. The important thing to remember is that these genetic injuries are small and new to the genome (unlike injuries in which an entire gene or part of a chromosome is missing or faulty), and the damage in these new, tiny mutations is not passed down from parent to child.

Some scientists believe that a substantial fraction of ASD cases involve widespread spontaneous genetic damage. What causes this damage, which doesn't show up in the parents? And what prevents the child's body from repairing it? In my opinion, autism is a disease with genetic injury that is also passed on, in many cases, via an abnormal genetic method of metabolizing vitamin D; in other words, both genetic injury and genetic inheritance are present. These types of mutations usually arise during times of rapid DNA division and occur at one of these three stages:

- *In the Father's Sperm:* Sperm are constantly replicating from birth, and a man is at risk for passing on damaged genes unless his DNA repair system is working. Studies show that older fathers are more likely than younger ones to have autistic children.[3] This is because an older man's DNA repair systems don't work as well as a younger man's systems.

- *During Pregnancy:* Fetal cells are constantly making copies of themselves, which are then exposed to a broad range of damage. Damage can occur when a pregnant woman takes valproic acid, for example. Valproic acid, or Depakote, which is associated with ASD and genetic damage (although valproic acid may cause a tiny percentage of autism), is used to treat epilepsy and stabilize mood. Valproic acid is also one of the few drugs known to reduce vitamin D levels. When a pregnant woman takes valproic acid and her child develops ASD, the genetic damage appears to occur during the first several months of pregnancy.

- *During Early Childhood:* At this stage, rapid cellular replication continues, especially in the brain. It seems likely that healthy toddlers with childhood disintegrative disorder suffer a brain injury early in childhood. Their disease may be separate from childhood autism, in which abnormalities appear shortly after birth.

Quite a few parents report entirely normal development of their children until about 12–18 months, when ASD symptoms rapidly appear. Other parents feel something is not right during the first few weeks of life. Different theories of autism have difficulty explaining why some children appear to be born with autistic symptoms and others experience them only after a period of normal development.

Epigenetics

If many cases of ASD are associated with a new genetic injury, what is injuring the genes? Some ASD geneticists believe that genetic/environmental interactions shared between parent and child are the only possible explanation for the ASD epidemic. This brings into the discussion the new but rapidly growing field of epigenetics,[4] which is the study of genetic changes that occur outside of the commonly understood concept of genetic inheritance. Epigenetics controls gene expression not by changing the DNA sequence but by changing which genes are expressed and thus the phenotype. For example, starvation modifies the expression of a given set of genes so that some genes can be expressed (turned into proteins) and others cannot.

Because epigenetic changes are affected by environmental factors, not classical genetic ones, ASD may also be caused by environmental factors (e.g., vitamin D deficiency) via an epigenetic pathway. The study of epigenetics and autism is an entirely new field, and little research has addressed it, although we know that vitamin D has an important role in epigenetics.[5]

COMMON SYMPTOMS OF VITAMIN D DEFICIENCY

weak bones	low energy and fatigue
sleep irregularities	muscle pain
lowered immunity	depression

THEORY 3: VACCINATIONS CAUSE AUTISM

Perhaps the single most popular explanation for autism among celebrities and many parents is childhood vaccines. No one can deny that, parallel to the autism epidemic, the number of vaccines we give our kids has skyrocketed. Instead of the five or six childhood vaccinations common in the 1970s, a child today might receive 25 different vaccinations. Moreover, many parents report watching their children deteriorate soon after receiving their 12- to 18-month vaccinations. Because a number of parents first become aware of autistic symptoms in their children around the time of routine vaccinations, they become understandably convinced that the vaccinations caused the ASD. Research, however, doesn't back up this theory. Scientists have spent hundreds of millions of dollars on vaccine and autism research, and the largest studies have found no association between the two.

In addition, the vaccine theory of ASD, like many theories eventually shown to be false, has a shifting hypothesis, a changing proposed explanation for a phenomenon such as a disease. First, the belief was that measles, mumps, and rubella (MMR) vaccine caused autism; then it was that a vaccine preservative, such as mercury, caused autism. After vaccine companies took mercury out of vaccines and the ASD epidemic continued to increase, vaccine opponents shifted their theory, blaming multiple vaccines given at one time—a more difficult hypothesis to test. Thus, when one vaccine theory is proven false, vaccine opponents just shift to another vaccine or vaccine component as the cause of autism.

Shifting hypotheses are signs of a strong sociological belief—not evidence of strong science.

The physician who first put forward the vaccine theory has been discredited for fraudulent work on his study, which actually may have been designed to make money.[6] In fact, his medical license has been restricted, and the medical journal that published his paper, *Lancet,* retracted his article after the fraud was exposed.[7] However, the tragedy of this is not that a doctor was discredited: it's that his fraudulent work wasn't exposed sooner. By the time of the article's retraction, celebrities such as Jenny McCarthy had begun promoting his false findings, and thousands and thousands of parents who believed that vaccines cause ASD didn't get their kids immunized at all. Predictably, outbreaks of serious yet preventable diseases, such as measles, have followed—and children have needlessly died because of an unproven theory.

> Scientists have spent hundreds of millions of dollars on vaccine and autism research, and the largest studies have found no association between the two.

Fortunately, evidence suggests that parents are shifting back toward accepting vaccines for their children.[8] I believe that children get autism whether they are vaccinated or not if they are

a. genetically predisposed,
b. have genetically abnormal vitamin D metabolism, and
c. are vitamin D–deficient.

This explains why most studies show that the rate of autism is the same in vaccinated and unvaccinated children.[9,10]

THEORY 4: UNCONTROLLED INFLAMMATION CAUSES AUTISM

The theory of unregulated inflammation causing autism is rapidly gaining ground as the race to solve the autism puzzle accelerates.[11] Unregulated inflammation occurs when the body can't properly control cellular irritation. It is usually triggered by an infection, toxin, or other noxious event. For example, if a pregnant woman's uterus becomes infected, inflammation results. If her body's immune system isn't working properly, the inflammation can become generalized and overwhelm the body. This situation can lead to unusual immune activation, which leads to an intense inflammatory reaction in the fetus—a risk factor for brain damage.[12] Vitamin D serves as an immune system modulator that reduces inflammation while enhancing protective immune responses.[13]

Of particular interest are excessive cytokines, small protein molecules that communicate the presence of inflammation to the immune system. A few cytokines prevent inflammation (are anti-inflammatory), but most promote inflammation. The presence of excessive cytokines in newborns is evidence of immune dysfunction that begins during pregnancy.[14] Studies have also connected infection during pregnancy with autism.[15] As you will see, studies of brain fluid and blood and microscopic studies of brains of autistic children who have died from other causes often reveal an inflammatory state. Vitamin D deficiency also leads to a hyper-inflammatory state (a heightened state of inflammation that can lead to different diseases), because vitamin D itself is both anti-infective and anti-inflammatory.

THEORY 5: AUTOIMMUNE DISEASE CAUSES AUTISM

The autoimmune theory is similar to the inflammation theory. The autoimmune phenomenon also occurs through inflammation when the body attacks itself. The cause of autoimmune diseases is still unknown, but genetic, infectious, inflammatory, and environmental factors likely all have a role. Many environmental factors (e.g., toxins, infections) can trigger the immune system to attack part of the body (e.g., the brain), and an autoimmune disease occurs.[16] Vitamin D deficiency has been associated with most autoimmune diseases, a fact few autism researchers seem to know.[17] More and more, scientists think vitamin D will be an effective treatment in at least some autoimmune disorders.[18]

> The cause of autoimmune diseases is still unknown, but genetic, infectious, inflammatory, and environmental factors likely all have a role.

THEORY 6: MITOCHONDRIAL DISEASE CAUSES AUTISM

Mitochondria are small structures inside cells that produce adenosine triphosphate (ATP), which transports chemical energy within cells for metabolism. Mitochondria are the power plants of cells.

One of the most recent theories, the mitochondrial theory, is based on data suggesting that deficient mitochondrial energy production is a feature of autism.[19] Mitochondrial disease is known to be a rare cause of autism, because inherited mitochondrial disorders, which are also rare, may be present, along with difficulty exercising, seizures, cognitive decline, and autistic characteristics.[20] Finding mitochondrial abnormalities in autism does not prove that a mitochondrial disorder is the cause; it can be the effect rather than the cause.[21] Recent studies have shown that steroids such as activated vitamin D activate genes in the mitochondria, as shown by vitamin D appearing to improve mitochondrial function.[22]

THEORY 7: TOXINS CAUSE AUTISM

Toxins are poisonous heavy metals such as mercury, nickel, and cadmium; solvents such as vinyl chloride; and a seemingly endless list of chemicals. All toxins can damage our genome if, as Harvard geneticist Dennis Kinney says, the usual defender of DNA (vitamin D) is not present in adequate amounts.[23] According to Kinney, without vitamin D, heavy metals and toxins are free to damage our genome, causing the new mutations so often found in autism and other illnesses.

Toxins that damage the genome are everywhere and, contrary to popular opinion, were much worse in the 1950s and 1960s, before the 1963 Clean Air Act. I am old enough to remember actually seeing the air I was breathing, watching rivers burn, and swimming in crystal-clear lakes that were dead due to acid rain. So, if autism is caused by pollutants in the air and water, the epidemic should have occurred when air and water pollution was at its worst, from the 1950s to the 1970s. It didn't.

Philip Landrigan, director of the Children's Environmental Health Center at the Mount Sinai School of Medicine, New York, and several colleagues, recently listed 10 chemicals found in consumer products that they suspect contribute to autism.[24] However, all 10 of the chemicals were in heavy use before the autism epidemic; in fact, in most cases, they are used much less since the epidemic began. That is not to say they are safe—only that the chemicals alone could not have caused the epidemic. However, in combination with a genetically prone child with a weakened immune system, they certainly could be culprits. If they are, and since they have been heavily used for many decades, what is the cause: the chemicals or the weakened immune system?

> To stay healthy, the body must have a built-in repair system. And, lucky for us, it does.

Toxins are everywhere. Every five days, simply by living on Earth, your body receives the same amount of ionizing radiation that it would get from a chest X-ray. Ionizing radiation is a particularly damaging form of radiation that can break chemical bonds in the body, creating highly reactive ions that can lead to genetic mutations. Many of these chemicals occur in nature: mercury, lead, arsenic, and cadmium. Even the clear, cold, pristine spring water gurgling from the ground—water we think of as pure—can harbor high concentrations of these dangerous heavy metals.

Perhaps more important, you are on fire; you are oxidizing. That's right. You are slowly burning food to stay alive, and the products of that combustion are particularly damaging to your genome. Even if you stopped eating, the process would continue as your body burned fat and muscle to stay alive.

Therefore, every day, many different toxins—chemicals, byproducts of combustion, viruses, heavy metals, radon from the earth, and X-rays—are damaging your genome. All these toxins work toward chaos, especially for your DNA, because all can cause DNA mutations. To stay healthy, the body must have a built-in repair system. And, lucky for us, it does.

DNA repair refers to the way a cell recognizes and repairs damage to its DNA. In human cells, normal oxidation, toxins, chemicals, and background radiation all damage DNA, resulting in as many as one million injuries per cell per day.[25] This sounds scary—and it is—but it goes to show how important DNA repair proteins are. And, keep in mind, the human body is composed of 3.7 trillion individual cells.[26] With so many injuries to the DNA of so many cells, sometimes it's hard to imagine how our bodies are capable of repairing it.

Sometimes the DNA is damaged to the point that it can no longer transcribe its message or use the DNA message to produce RNA (ribonucleic acid), which then produces proteins and other substances needed for life. Other substances prompt harmful modifications in the cell's genome, affecting the survival of daughter cells after the cell splits. Therefore, a robust DNA repair process is constantly occurring. When normal repair processes fail, and when normal cell death does not end the injury, irreparable mutations are likely. As I discuss in Chapter Eight, vitamin D is intimately involved with DNA repair in that it regulates the genes needed to make DNA repair proteins.

> In human cells, normal oxidation, toxins, chemicals, and background radiation all damage DNA, resulting in as many as one million injuries per cell per day.[25]

THEORY 8: SEROTONIN AND BRAIN DEVELOPMENT

The serotonin hypothesis attempts to explain why peripheral blood levels of serotonin tend to be high in ASD, while central brain serotonin concentrations are low.[27] This is called the serotonin paradox. In the brain, serotonin is not just a neurotransmitter; it is involved in brain growth and development. Serotonin acts as a growth factor during early brain development, and serotonin receptor activity plays a crucial part in the series of events that leads to changes in brain structure. Very recently, two scientists at the University of California at Berkeley (one is a member of the National Academy of Sciences) discovered that vitamin D entirely explains the serotonin parodox.[28]

ONE DISORDER, MULTIPLE THEORIES

So we have multiple theories for the same disorder—some radically different. However, they all describe a biochemical event or an injury that the body didn't repair or that triggered a systemic response. Children with these changes are at increased risk for autism.

The lingering questions are:

a. What, exactly, is this event or injury, and what causes it?,
b. Is there an underlying immune system dysregulation?, and
c. Why do so many of our children have it?

If we can answer those questions, we will be on the path to being able to do something about it.

CHAPTER THREE

AUTISM: A NEW THEORY

Over the past 20 years, scientists have assured us that effective prevention and treatment of autism are just a matter of time. However, as time passes, the epidemic shows no signs of abating. A recent *Forbes* article reports that, in the next decade, half a million US children with autism will become adults, ballooning the number of autistic adults by 50 percent.[1] The same article reports that most young autistic adults spend their days in adult daycare; only 18 percent are employed, and even fewer live independently.

If the Centers for Disease Control and Prevention's (CDC's) worst-case scenario of a 12 percent yearly increase in the incidence of autism proves to be true, we will be in serious trouble in terms of caring for these individuals.[2] It's time to look at autism a new way—with a new theory.

MY VIEW OF AUTISM

In October 2007, I published a paper in the British journal *Medical Hypotheses* that proposed a completely new explanation for autism.[3] I argued that autism was not caused by a toxin, virus, vaccine, solvent, or classic genetic mutation. Instead, I proposed that autism is the result of:

a. a predisposing genetic abnormality in the way the body processes vitamin D,

b. a noxious triggering event, and

c. a dramatic and very recent epidemic of vitamin D deficiency.

This combination injures the built-in repair systems the human body has developed over two million years to protect against and repair cellular injuries.[4]

Remember, whether injuries such as small mutations pop up from background radiation, inflammation, or the products of combustion or toxins, the immune system must be able to prevent and repair the damage. I wondered whether the immune system could have suffered a dramatic injury over the past 30 years.

In my article, I argued that the genetics of the vitamin D system (all the body's "machinery" that goes into making vitamin D) could explain autism. I realized that, instead of severe mutations in the vitamin D system, genetic variations in the body's capacity to metabolize vitamin D *plus* vitamin D deficiency could explain autism. That is, if you inherited only a little of the enzyme that turns vitamin D into a steroid hormone *and* you also weren't getting enough vitamin D, these two problems together would keep your brain from getting the activated vitamin D it needs to develop.

> Vitamin D is in charge of increasing the number of proteins made in the body to repair its own DNA.

On the other hand, if you inherited a lot of the enzyme that activates vitamin D or many vitamin D receptors (that increase uptake of vitamin D), your brain would be able to get most of the vitamin D it needs.

This, I believe, is why autism has been passed down for ages from parent to child without harm—but the disorder's incidence rate has exploded only since the emergence of the vitamin D deficiency epidemic.

More important, my 2007 paper explored autism from the viewpoint that the best theory is the one that can explain the most facts in the simplest manner; that is, one theory explaining eight facts is much better than eight different theories explaining eight different facts.[3] Three years later, I updated my vitamin D theory of autism in the 90-year-old journal *Acta Paediatrica.*[5] Furthermore, I now conclude that the genetic injuries in autism—the small, new point mutations—are the *effects* and not the *causes* of autism. Vitamin D is in charge of increasing the number of proteins made in the body to repair its own DNA. Thus, vitamin D deficiency prevents repair of these ongoing genetic injuries.

LIFE WITHOUT SUNSHINE

Our body's natural ability to defend itself against assaults has been stripped of its effectiveness by perhaps the worst advice physicians have ever given: stay out of the sun. That well-meaning advice should have been followed by a caveat to take extra vitamin D to make up for what the sun no longer makes in your skin, or to expose your skin to the sun for 15 minutes per day.

One of the world's leading researchers on vitamin D, Michael Holick of Boston University, writing in *The New England Journal of Medicine,* contends that this sun avoidance advice has contributed heavily to what he now calls the vitamin D deficiency epidemic, which has greatly impaired our immune systems, or our ability to fight off disease.[6]

♦

THE SUN SCARE

Sun avoidance was common in other eras and places, such as in Victorian England, where women wore long dresses and carried parasols. Fair skin was an indicator of wealth, a sign that you were not a laborer. We have no record of autism from that time. Remember, the women avoiding the sun in that era were a tiny wealthy minority. And certainly no one, including the wealthy, slathered themselves or their children with sunscreen.

Just a few decades ago, we had no sunscreen and no fear of the sun. Mothers told their kids that fresh air and sunshine would do them good. In fact, in the 1920s, the American Medical Association (AMA) recommended sun exposure for a wide variety of ailments.[7] By that time, certain wavelengths emitted by electric lights were also known to fight infections.

The 1929 edition of the *Encyclopedia Britannica* summarized the mechanism of action known at the time[8]: "As has been shown in the irradiation of the skin with ultraviolet light, the light of the electric arc, and sunlight that by these agencies also the bactericidal power of the blood is increased. . . . It is not yet known how irradiation produces these results."

In the 1920s and 1930s, artificial sunlight and sunbathing in open-air solariums were widely used as effective treatments for general health problems and a variety of bacterial and viral illnesses. For evidence of how people viewed infantile sun exposure in the United States in the 1930s, when autism was rare, the following are a few quotes from the 1931 pamphlet from the US Department of Agriculture, *Sunlight for Babies*[9]:

"A child needs the sun most when he is growing fastest—in babyhood and early childhood."

"Every mother who wishes her baby to have robust health should give him regular sunbaths from early infancy until he is old enough to play in the sun himself."

"The baby should get tanned all over, but the tanning should take place gradually."

"Older children, as well as babies, need plenty of sunlight."

SIX SEEMINGLY UNRELATED FACTS ABOUT AUTISM

The best scientific theory is one that can explain the most facts in the simplest manner. Let's take a quick look at six facts about autism and the six different theories of the scientists who discovered the facts. To quote Sir Isaac Newton, "We are to admit no more causes of natural things than such as are both true and sufficient to explain their appearances. Therefore, to the same natural effects we must, so far as possible, assign the same causes."[10]

Fact 1: Autism has increased dramatically

Most experts now agree that autism has risen alarmingly over the past 30 years. The scientists believing this fact thought that some unidentified environmental agent introduced during this time (such as a new vaccine) was causing the epidemic. Although most scientists believe the vaccination theory incorrect, many parents still believe it, especially those who watched their normal toddlers deteriorate at 12–18 months—about the time they received their vaccinations.

Certainly, the number of vaccinations our children receive has increased dramatically during the past 30 years.

So, as our first example, we have one fact (a rapid increase in cases of autism) and one theory (vaccinations) to explain it.

Fact 2: Autism is more common in polluted areas

Several studies have shown that autism is more common in areas with polluted air, due to the toxic effect of pollutants on developing fetal brains.[11,12] This theory makes sense because a number of toxins can damage genes. According to the researchers, pregnant women and young children living in polluted air have more toxins in their brains.

The theory of toxins in air pollution explains Fact 2. Notice that we have two facts and two entirely different theories.

Fact 3: Autism is more common in cloudy and rainy areas

According to research by Michael Waldman and colleagues at Cornell University, the greater incidence of autism in areas with more clouds and rain, where children are more likely to take part in indoor activities, is due to the increased use of electronic devices in rainy and cloudy areas and the effect these devices have on the brains of developing children.[13]

Certainly, these devices have proliferated over the past 30 years, so perhaps they are emitting radiation that damages fetal and young children's brains, causing autism.

Now we have three facts and three entirely different theories. So do we stop vaccinating our children, clean our air, or throw away our cell phones?

Fact 4: Autistic boys have thin bones

The cortex, or outer covering, of bones of autistic boys is thinner than in the bones of normal children, which some researchers say is due to the eccentric diets of many autistic children.[14] Certainly, children with autism often have unusual diets, especially those with no milk products, so a lack of calcium could certainly explain this finding. However, some unidentified toxin may be damaging both bones and brains.

Four facts, four theories.

Fact 5: Autism is more common in wealthy, educated white families

The incidence of autism is higher among better-educated and richer white families[15] than it is among poor, less-educated white families. According to some studies, this is because better-educated and richer parents seek treatment for their children more often.

The finding that autism is more common in families with higher incomes and better educations is one of the most unusual and hotly debated issues about autism.

Other than a statistical fluke, what could explain such an unusual fact?[16]

Fact 6: Autism is more common in dark-skinned people

Some, but not all, studies show that autism is more common in blacks than in whites.[17–22] However, some scientists believe those findings are due to underdetection among the poor and failure to correct for socio-economic status. For example, Bruce Ames, a member of the National Academy of Science, reports that CDC data show that the prevalence of autism among wealthy black children is twice as high as it is for wealthy white children.[23]

Some experts cite the same reasons most diseases are more common in blacks than in whites: poverty and poor prenatal care. Certainly, heart disease, most cancers, pneumonia, hypertension, diabetes, and autoimmune diseases are more common among blacks than whites. So why not autism? A CDC study found that black children in Atlanta were almost twice as likely to have autism—and more severe autism—than white children.[16]

There is no name in the Somali language for autism, but in Minnesota, home to many dark-skinned Somali immigrants, Somalis call autism the "Minnesota disease." Somalis in Sweden call it the "Swedish disease."

So we have our sixth fact and our sixth different explanation: autism is more common among dark-skinned people, perhaps due to poor prenatal care.

Are Improvements Related to Vitamin D Supplementation Long-Lasting?

Dear Dr. Cannell:

My three-year-old child has autism spectrum disorder, apraxia of speech, and hypotonia. I visited your website about autism and vitamin D deficiency and shared the information with our pediatrician. He was willing to try high doses of vitamin D, provided we tested blood levels monthly.

We started giving our son 4,000 IU of vitamin D daily. A week and a half before his first blood test, I started taking him out in the sun for 20–30 minutes per day. His vitamin D level was 51 ng/mL [normal is 30–75 ng/mL]. At first, we noticed more hitting, biting, and temper tantrums, but this passed after a week.

After two weeks, his vitamin D level increased to 64.8 ng/mL. We noticed small improvements in his behavior, such as less stimming and fewer tantrums.

After four weeks, we saw bursts of spontaneous language. He started asking questions and starting conversations. The hitting, biting, and temper tantrums went away. He started pedaling his tricycle, which he had been too uncoordinated to do before.

After six months, his vitamin D level is now 84 ng/mL. His speech continues to improve, and he uses complete sentences in a tone that is no longer monotone and robotic. Most important, for the first time, he seems happy.

We can't believe it, and his doctor can't either. Will these improvements continue?

Yours truly,
Amanda

Dear Amanda:

I am so happy for you and your child. As far as the improvements go, I don't know if they will continue, but I suspect the improvements will last as long as his vitamin D level remains in the high part of the range you described.

John Cannell, MD

Can A Single Theory Explain All Six Facts?

Scientists explain the six different facts outlined above using six entirely different but completely tenable theories. Can one theory alone explain all six of these facts? If so, such a theory is the best theory because it is the most prudent, economical, reasonable, and encompassing.

Here's the theory: Autism is caused by vitamin D deficiency during pregnancy or early childhood. Let's see if it can explain these six seemingly unconnected facts.

Fact 1: Autism has increased dramatically

The rapid increase in the incidence of autism since the late 1980s coincides almost perfectly with the timing of the "sun scare," with the medical profession advising people to protect themselves from skin cancer by staying out of the sun or using sunscreen, which also blocks vitamin D absorption.[24] (Ultraviolet light in sunshine is now listed by the US government as a toxin.[25])

Although we have no studies that show changes in vitamin D levels over the past 30 years, the average vitamin D level in the United States in 1988 was 30 ng/mL; by 2001, it was only 24 ng/mL.[26] Likewise, the prevalence of extremely low vitamin D levels (less than 10 ng/mL) tripled during the same period. In Denmark, where they keep better records on vitamin D, vitamin D levels have fallen even more dramatically. Average vitamin D levels decreased from 25 ng/mL in 1994 to 20 ng/mL in 2001 and to 17 ng/mL in 2008.[27,28]

Could the vitamin D deficiency epidemic explain the epidemic of autism?

Fact 2: Autism is more common in polluted areas

This fact is explained by a well-conducted study that showed that air pollution reduces the amount of vitamin D–producing ultraviolet B (UVB) radiation from sunlight penetrating the atmosphere, lowering vitamin D absorption in pregnant women and thus lowering their infants' vitamin D levels.[29] However, some UVB still gets through polluted air, so the rate of autism should be only slightly increased in polluted areas—which is the case.

Fact 3: Autism is more common in cloudy and rainy areas

Cloudy and rainy areas have a higher prevalence of autism. Those same clouds and rain greatly impair penetration of vitamin D–producing UVB light, lowering vitamin D production. People who live in cloudy and rainy areas have lower vitamin D levels than people who live in sunny areas due to clouds impairing vitamin D production in the skin. Also, people who live in rainy areas are more likely to spend more time inside, further lowering their vitamin D levels.

Fact 4: Autistic boys have thin bones

Simply put, vitamin D deficiency during pregnancy or early childhood results in thin bones—and lays the environmental groundwork for autism.[30]

Fact 5: Autism is more common in wealthy, educated white families

This fact (which does not apply to nearly any other disease) is explained by studies that show that wealthy, educated parents are more likely to practice sun avoidance and apply sunscreen than are low-income, less-educated parents. They are also less likely to allow unprotected sun exposure for young children[31] and pregnant women.[32] This situation results in lower vitamin D levels during crucial periods of brain development and, potentially, more autism.

Fact 6: Autism is more common in dark-skinned people

Although controversial and not supported by all studies,[33] this fact is also explained by the vitamin D theory. Melanin is a skin-darkening pigment that also acts as an effective sunscreen. As a result, people with a lot of melanin in their skin have low vitamin D levels. In fact, many black women of childbearing age have virtually no detectable vitamin D in their blood, meaning their babies develop in an extremely vitamin D–poor environment.[34]

So our one test theory explains all six facts. Few theories can explain six facts about any disease without assuming some beliefs to be true. A principle known as Occam's razor generally recommends choosing from competing possible explanations the theory that makes the fewest assumptions (in other words, the one based on facts rather than beliefs that may or may not be true). So far, we have not had to make *any* new assumptions for the vitamin D theory of autism.

◆

THE UN-AUTISTIC SYNDROME

Studying Williams syndrome,[35] which is a rare genetic syndrome, has allowed scientists to examine a theory about autism. Articles in *The New England Journal of Medicine* and other journals have documented that fetuses and very young infants with Williams syndrome have exceptionally high blood levels of activated vitamin D. [36,37]

Children with Williams syndrome have outgoing personalities, perhaps because their brains were flooded with vitamin D during certain stages of brain development. These children are not shy around strangers, make good eye contact, and are engaging and social. Sometimes they get in trouble by making friends with strangers.

Because the personalities of many children with Williams syndrome are often the opposite of those of autistic children,[38] Williams syndrome has been nicknamed the "Un-Autistic Syndrome."

CHAPTER FOUR

MESSING WITH MOTHER NATURE

Vitamin D helps regulate 1,000–2,000 genes, about 5–10 percent of the active human genome, either increasing (upregulating) or decreasing (downregulating) the amount of protein that the gene makes, according to the body's needs.[1] Most people the world over are vitamin D–deficient and missing out on all the other benefits of exposure to the ultraviolet B band of sunlight.

Because I believe that sun exposure should be an integral part of an autistic child's treatment, this chapter describes how our bodies make vitamin D and discusses the pros and cons of sun exposure. Is vitamin D the only good thing the sun does for you? Is it safe to mess with Mother Nature and get all your sunshine from a bottle of vitamin D? What about the risk of disfiguring—and sometimes deadly—skin cancer?

HERE COMES THE SUNSCREEN

Fortunately, safe sun exposure of as few as 10 minutes per day is the easiest way to elevate vitamin D levels. If you go outside in a swimsuit for 10–20 minutes at about noon in summer, you will make about

10,000 units of vitamin D.[2] However, properly applied and reapplied sunscreen prevents most vitamin D production in the skin.[3] Although the bottle says to apply sunscreen before going in the sun, the Vitamin D Council recommends that you start with 5–20 minutes of full-body sunscreen-free sun exposure before applying sunscreen, depending on the lightness or darkness of your skin. As the summer progresses and the skin tans, you and your children can spend more time in the sun without sunscreen.

> The Vitamin D Council recommends that you start with 5–20 minutes of full-body sunscreen-free sun exposure before applying sunscreen.

For nearly two million years, humans lived naked in the sun around the equator. About 80,000 years ago, some of our ancestors began migrating from the equator to northern and southern latitudes. Even as recently as 10,000 years ago, few people wore clothes, except to keep warm. Our ancestors who lived in Europe and places with similar climates wore few clothes during the hot summers, storing large amounts of vitamin D in their fat and muscles for use during winter. Until about 300 years ago, most common people worked, gardened, and walked outside, making large quantities of vitamin D in the summer.

However, with the Industrial Revolution, more people started working indoors, which limited their exposure to the sun. Around this time, the "diseases of civilization," such as heart disease, cancer, and diabetes, dramatically increased.[4] About 100 years ago, we began traveling in cars with glass (which blocks all vitamin D production by sunlight) instead of walking or riding horses, further insulating us from sunlight.

As recently as 75 years ago, many people eagerly sought the sun for health reasons. Parents knew that children needed fresh air and sunlight to thrive. The same mindset was true in hospital settings. Tuberculosis treatment in sanatoriums, for example, usually included deliberate and frequent sun exposure.

By 1925, the AMA was comfortable enough with the scientific evidence of the antituberculin properties of vitamin D to issue the following statement: "The benefit derived by patients suffering from tuberculosis of the bones, articulations, peritoneum, intestine, larynx, and lymph nodes when exposed to natural sunlight or to the rays emitted by certain artificial sources of radiation cannot be doubted . . ."[5]

About 40 years ago, we began using sunscreen and avoiding the sun in deadly earnest. Now, many people intentionally avoid the sun based on what I consider very poor advice.

In the past 30 years, we also have seen the three childhood epidemics of autism, asthma, and food allergies.[6,7] Until the recent public health campaigns to persuade us to avoid the sun and wear sunscreen, many people's bodies produced ample amounts of vitamin D in the skin in the summer and then stored it in muscles and fat for use in winter.

HOW OUR BODIES MAKE VITAMIN D

Can you get all the vitamins you need just from your diet? No. You'll notice that I deliberately call vitamin D a *system*. The entire system for making vitamin D is in the skin; in the natural world, any vitamin D you get from food is largely incidental. The vitamin D system activates when sunlight strikes the skin, turning a cholesterol-type molecule into pre-vitamin D, an intermediate in the production of vitamin D. Using heat in the skin, pre-vitamin D becomes vitamin D. That is, the final reaction to make vitamin D is heat-driven—the more heat in the skin, the more vitamin D.

The Mountain Pool

Before we get back to the sun, let's briefly look at the path vitamin D takes in the body. The liver transforms vitamin D into calcidiol, or 25(OH)D, which is used as a building block to create the activated vitamin D steroid hormone known as calcitriol, or 1,25(OH)2D. The kidney uses calcidiol to make blood calcitriol for maintaining blood calcium levels; this is the most immediate life-sustaining endocrine function of vitamin D, because if your blood calcium levels fall too low, you die.

It helps to think of vitamin D as a large mountain pool that flows into other smaller pools below it. The top pool consists of calcidiol. If calcidiol levels in the top pool fall too low, your kidneys can't make enough blood calcitriol, your calcium level drops too low, and you die because your heart does not have enough calcium to make it beat. If you don't have enough vitamin D to perform more than this function, the upper pool (the blood-calcium function) takes precedence over everything else and claims almost all available vitamin D.

Below the top pool are hundreds of other pools that might help prevent cancer, heart disease, influenza, multiple sclerosis (a disabling autoimmune disease), chronic pain, autism, or depression. If you have enough calcidiol, it fills the pool for the kidneys and all the other pools below it. If there is enough calcidiol, trillions of cells in your body can turn calcidiol into calcitriol (the steroid hormone that turns genes on and off)—but only if they need it. That last point is crucial: the cells in the tissues involved make the steroid hormone calcitriol only if they need it; otherwise, the body gets rid of any extra vitamin D via the kidneys.

Now let's look at vitamin A, another vitamin hormone that triggers genes. The vitamin A you take in pill form is not a building block but rather the hormone itself. That's why we see so much toxicity of vitamin A in the United States; people take the hormone rather than the building block, and the body has trouble regulating this form.[8]

Studies of ASD children show they have excessive vitamin A intake.[9] The average American takes in more vitamin A than the government recommends.[10] When you take vitamin A supplements, you bypass your body's regulatory system and dump the vitamin A hormone directly into tissues.

Scientists have yet to fully discover how rapidly the body gets rid of extra vitamin A. Vitamin D is available

The cells in the tissues involved make the steroid hormone calcitriol only if they need it; otherwise, the body gets rid of any extra vitamin D via the kidneys.

for cells only if they need it. But because the body is so efficient at getting rid of extra vitamin D through the urinary and the gastrointestinal (stomach) tracts, you would overdose on vitamin D only if you daily took tens of thousands of units for months or even years.

From our mountain pool analogy, if some lower pools are empty or nearly so, the tissue they feed cannot make enough calcitriol (activated vitamin D). If the pools are full, the tissues make and use activated vitamin D to turn genes on and off in response to a wide variety of conditions. As with some other pools, I suspect that vitamin D completely fills the pool for autism prevention only when vitamin D levels are in the natural range (about 50 ng/ mL). This can happen only if the big pool at the top of the mountain is full.

Who Drained the Pool?

Most of our personal pools probably aren't full because we don't get enough sunlight. Vitamin D deficiency started about 40 years ago, when the cosmetics industry realized it could increase sales by going beyond beauty issues to target health concerns.[11]

The cosmetic industry knew that some studies showed that sunlight was associated with skin cancer. The industry took the obvious step and put sunscreen into cosmetic products and then began warning people that even moderate amounts of sunlight were dangerous—if the sun didn't cause skin cancer, it would most certainly cause wrinkles.[12] (The wrinkles many people fear from sunlight, such as those found on elderly sea captains, occur with *excessive* sun exposure.)

Cosmetic firms then funded dermatology departments at major universities, which began to warn people about the dangers of sunshine.[13] It worked. In 1989, the AMA and other groups began telling pregnant women and children to completely avoid the sun, without mentioning how to get enough vitamin D. This was radical advice, given that the

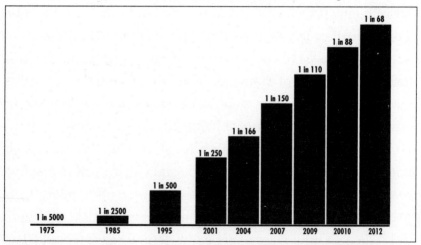

According to studies by Autism Speaks (www.AutismSpeaks.org), there has been a dramatic increase in the prevalence of autism since 1975. Some of the increase may be due to changes in diagnostic practices, and some may be influenced by environmental factors.

body needs the sun to make vitamin D. Sales jumped from $18 million in 1972 to $500 million in 1996 and are still growing.[14] Also, sales of sun-protective clothing boomed between 1992 and 2002.[15] Meanwhile, the autism epidemic exploded.

Sun Avoidance and Death

If you asked 100 people whether sun exposure made you die younger than you otherwise would, 99 of them

> 400,000 American lives would be saved every year if Americans sunbathed on a regular basis.

would answer yes. However, a very recent study in the *Journal of Internal Medicine* found just the opposite. This 2014 Swedish study of 30,000 women showed that those who completely avoided the sun were twice as likely to die during the 20 years of the study as those who suntanned, went on vacations to sunny areas, and avoided using sunscreen.[16] In fact, in an overlooked portion of the study, women who used suntanning booths were less likely to die than women who did not.

William Grant accurately predicted the findings of this Swedish study in 2009 when he wrote that 400,000 American lives would be saved every year if Americans sunbathed on a regular basis.[17]

The Sun and Skin Cancer

People are rightfully concerned about the sun and the role it plays in skin cancer, especially melanoma, a deadly type of skin cancer. Although too much sun may indeed cause squamous cell carcinoma and basal cell carcinoma, these non-melanoma skin cancers are highly treatable with regular dermatological care, although people who have either have an elevated likelihood of a recurrence. Many dermatologists just burn or freeze them off. In fact, these skin cancers are so common, they are not listed in most cancer databases. However, if you do not seek medical care, these cancers grow and can kill you. About 1,500 Americans die every year from these non-melanoma skin cancers.

Ask most Americans if the sun causes cancer, and they quickly say yes. Then ask them if the sun prevents cancer, and they are confused. If you tell them that they are much more likely to die from cancer if they totally avoid the sun, they probably won't believe you—but you'd be right.[18]

Actually, there's good evidence that the sun both causes *and* prevents common skin cancers.[19] The ultraviolet radiation (potentially damaging radiation) in sunlight certainly can damage skin cells of vitamin D–deficient people, causing their skin to age. Some damaged skin cells may turn into skin cancers; studies show this usually occurs after people reach retirement age.

The skin is one of the few organs that can make activated vitamin D directly from the sun without going through the liver.[20] This ability to make activated vitamin D means nature's best cancer fighter is available to fix sun-damaged cells immediately if you are regularly exposed to the sun. If you get even less sun in retirement, however, activated vitamin D is not available to fight skin cancer. The skin is already damaged from the sun and in need of vitamin D.

Vitamin D + Sunlight = Powerful Anticancer Protection

Most people know about vitamin D's role in bone health, but that is only one of its many benefits. Activated vitamin D is also one of the most powerful anticancer substances known.[21] Through the production of vitamin D, sunlight helps prevent internal cancers, such as those of organs, blood, and tissues. It's as if Mother Nature knew we needed vitamin D to prevent internal cancers and that we would get skin cancer from the sun; therefore, she provided ready-made skin protection and chemotherapy (use of drugs to treat cancer) in the form of activated vitamin D. Now, modern medicine has made sunlight Public Enemy No. 1, encouraging us, in effect, to give up our protection from internal cancers and many other diseases.

When we look at skin cancer research, it's clear that avoiding excess sunlight, especially sunburns, does reduce the risk of squamous cell cancer. Sunlight's relationship with the other common skin cancer, basal cell carcinoma, is more complicated; however, chronic sun exposure probably does increase its incidence.

> Activated vitamin D is also one of the most powerful anticancer substances known.

One point that gets lost, however, is that sun exposure is only one risk factor for skin cancer. Diet is important, as is genetic tendency. Keep in mind that about 1,500 Americans die from squamous and basal cell carcinoma every year, while perhaps as many as 1,500 Americans die as a result of vitamin D deficiency *each day*.[22]

Furthermore, many people who have skin cancer worked or spent time outside for much of their active lives without getting skin cancer and then retired and began avoiding the sun. When they receive a diagnosis of non-melanoma skin cancer (usually on their faces, heads, or hands), their doctor tells them, quite rightly, that the total amount of sunlight they received over their lifetime—their radiation burden—was the culprit.

However, if they avoid the sun in retirement, something else happens: their vitamin D levels plummet. Without the sun, their bodies can no longer make activated vitamin D to fight skin cancer. Because 70 percent of vitamin D in most people comes from the sun rather than from diet or supplements, they have no easy way of replacing the vitamin D being lost. Years of chronic sun exposure and skin damage catch up with them, and subsequent sunlight deprivation reduces their natural cancer protection system.

THE MOST FEARED SKIN CANCER

The skin cancer we fear most is malignant melanoma, which kills about 9,700 Americans each year. However, the incidence of stage 1 melanoma has tripled over the past 40 years despite more people avoiding the sun and using sunscreen.[22] Why is this cancer increasing if so many people are taking sun precautions?

Although frequent severe sunburns, especially as a child, do increase the risk of melanoma, few people know that frequent sun exposure, without burning, actually *decreases* melanoma risk.[23] In fact, indoor workers are at higher risk than outdoor workers for melanoma.[24] In addition, melanomas are most likely to occur on areas of the body not routinely exposed to sunlight, such as the chest, back, and upper legs, although the face and neck are also common melanoma sites. [25]

Another fact about melanoma has recently come to light. Although the diagnosis of melanoma has been steadily increasing, melanoma death rates have not.[26] Dermatologists tell you that's because they are doing such a good job detecting and treating early melanoma. However, before you congratulate them, consider this: the only type of melanoma that has been increasing is stage 1 melanoma, or melanoma that has not spread beyond the skin. The more advanced cases of melanoma, such as those that spread to a lymph node (small, bean-shaped glands found throughout the body) or other organs, has increased little, if at all.

Recently, researchers from the Dermatology Department of the Norfolk and Norwich University Hospital in England published a paper titled "Melanoma Epidemic: A Midsummer Night's Dream?"[26] In it, they analyzed 3,971 cases of melanoma over 13 years and found that the increase in melanoma was almost entirely due to stage 1 disease. They showed that the diagnosis of melanoma had increased dramatically, but there was very little increase in metastatic (spreading, or no longer localized) melanoma and almost no increase in death rates.

The authors pointed out that a melanoma epidemic was an impossibility because such an epidemic would have to include higher rates of more advanced disease. They called for a reevaluation of the role of sunshine and a new direction in looking for the cause of melanoma. The number of moles, red hair, and heredity play the most important roles in melanoma.[27] Genetics have a particularly important role in malignant melanoma.[28]

This is not a new idea. In 1997, researchers from Emory University in Atlanta analyzed similar US data and issued the same warning, contending that little evidence suggested an increase in melanoma rates.[29] What is happening is simple: People are concerned about melanoma, so they go to their dermatologist more often when they see a change in a mole, or brown or black growth on the skin. The dermatologist obtains a biopsy, or sample of tissue, and sends it to a pathologist (a doctor who is an expert in diseases and the tissue changes they cause). Some pathologists probably ask themselves: "What happens if I say this is benign and I am wrong? Will I be sued?" Thus, the pathologist says the specimen is melanoma.

Dermatologists could easily test this idea by comparing slides of melanoma biopsies from the 1960s with melanoma slides from today. More and more scientists think such a study would show that more noncancerous lesions (any abnormality in tissues like skin) are diagnosed as melanoma today than in the past. In other words, in the 1960s, what was called a normal mole could today be called melanoma.

Don't misunderstand me. Sunburns do increase the risk of melanoma, and if you have risk factors for melanoma, such as a lot of moles, red hair, or family history, extra caution is indeed due. In fact, a recent review of risk factors for melanoma listed sunburn third; the five other important factors were number of moles, presence of freckles, history of sunburn, hair color, and skin color.[30] However, melanoma can occur inside the mouth, in the esophagus, on the penis, or inside the vagina, hardly areas of the body exposed to the sun.

As with the more benign forms of skin cancer, stage 1 melanoma might be increasing because vitamin D levels are falling—an idea that's finally starting to catch on. Prominent dermatologists at a major university in England warned that avoiding the sun may increase the risk of dying from melanoma by depleting vitamin D levels.[31]

PROCEED AT YOUR OWN PERIL

Besides slowing the aging of skin and preventing two forms of skin cancer, what else happens when you avoid the sun? Apparently, no one really thought about this question until recently. Now it's becoming increasingly clear that sunlight avoidance and the resulting vitamin D depletion increase the risk of dying from internal cancers by up to 50 percent.[32] When we avoid the sun, we are at greater risk for cancers of the colon, breast, and prostate.[33] In fact, people who spend less time in the sun are at higher risk for almost all fatal internal cancers than those who spend more time in the sun.[34-37]

Apparently, no organization or government agency with "avoid the sun" campaigns considered the possibility that avoiding the sun would harm anyone. No one remembered that humans evolved in the sun. Only in recent years did we start avoiding the sun. In other words, we started messing with Mother Nature. Furthermore, when the government and the AMA began to tell us to avoid the sun in the late 1980s, they forgot to tell us to take a vitamin D supplement to make up for the vitamin D we'd no longer be making.

> People who spend less time in the sun are at higher risk for almost all fatal internal cancers than those who spend more time in the sun.

VITAMIN D HELPED OUR SON USE LANGUAGE AGAIN

Dear Dr. Cannell:

My 19-year-old, 300-pound son Jacob has autism. He was born normal and was progressing ahead of schedule until age three, when he lost the ability to use language, make eye contact, focus, and regulate his behavior. In 2011, I started giving Jacob 1,000 IU vitamin D twice daily and, under his physician's care, increased his dose to 12,000 IU twice daily with food (to help him absorb the vitamin better).

After two months, his vitamin D blood level was 82 ng/mL [normal is 30–74 ng/mL]. He is now able to tell me about his day in detail. His language continues to improve, and he seems happy most days. He is not "cured," but I think he will be able to learn how to take care of himself after we are gone, and that is such a load off our minds. I don't know how to thank you.

Best, Perry

Dear Perry:

You are lucky that your doctor was willing to try it; many will not. At 82 ng/mL, your son's vitamin D level is similar to those *of some lifeguards at the end of summer or modern hunter-gatherers near the equator. His levels could theoretically be obtained in the natural state by sun exposure alone.*

At 300 pounds, 12,000 IU/day may be the correct dose, but continue having his doctor test his vitamin D level every three months. Also remember to get him outside in the late spring and summer without sunscreen in as few clothes as possible when his shadow is shorter than he is, being careful that he does not burn.

John Cannell, MD

What Else Does the Sun Give Us?

If you decide to just take a pill while completely avoiding the sun, you are assuming that science knows everything. What does ultraviolet sunlight do that science has yet to discover? Let me give you a couple examples.

- *Endorphin Production:* In 2013, a group from the University of Kentucky reviewed the substantial evidence that sunlight triggers the production of endorphins (naturally occurring morphine-like substances produced by the body) in the skin, the same kind of morphine-like molecules that you get from exercise.[38] That is one reason that sunlight and sun beds make you feel better. Another reason is that bright light improves mood, working through the retinas (light-sensitive layers of tissue lining the inner surface of the eye) and the pineal gland (a pea-size organ in the middle of the brain).

Why would nature reward you with a morphine-like substance for exercising? Because if it feels good, you're more likely to do it. Why would nature reward you with a morphine-like substance for exposing yourself to ultraviolet light? Maybe because it is also good for you, and nature wants you to do it. I can't understand why having a normal relationship with the sun has become such a radical idea.

Some dermatologists were so concerned that sunlight might make study subjects feel better via endorphins that they gave a narcotic blocker, naltrexone (the same drug given to narcotic addicts), to frequent indoor tanners and infrequent indoor tanner control subjects.[38]

They found that naltrexone reduced the use of sun beds by frequent tanners and that the tanners exhibited narcotic-like withdrawal symptoms. Strangely, the dermatologists concluded that suntanning is an addiction that should be treated like a narcotic habit. Their thinking must have been the following: "UV light makes you feel better, so it's an addiction and should be treated." Most practicing dermatologists have this attitude because they have been bombarded with one-sided information about the sun.

> Sunlight has beneficial effects on the immune system independent of vitamin D.

- *Slowing the Progression of Multiple Sclerosis:* Multiple sclerosis (MS) is a devastating neurological disease. Hector DeLuca of the University of Wisconsin (a giant in vitamin D research) was the first to discover that vitamin D slowed MS progression in lab animals.[39] Recently, DeLuca's lab discovered that continuous treatment with ultraviolet radiation of a wavelength that does not make vitamin D works even better.[40] He concluded that vitamin D supplementation alone could not replace sunlight in helping the immune system suppress MS in lab animals. That is, sunlight has beneficial effects on the immune system independent of vitamin D.[41]

THE SUN IS NOT RISK-FREE

Although I advocate sun exposure, I do so with a few warnings. Overexposure, or sunburn, is clearly dangerous. Sunburns increase the risk of melanoma and can also permanently change the melanin content of skin, creating marks such as freckles. Sunburns also age the skin and damage its collagen.

So, despite all of the good things the sun does, be aware of the risks of excessive sun exposure. Never allow yourself or your child to burn. Fair skin, a lot of moles (especially unusual ones), freckles, red hair, and a family history of melanoma are risk factors for melanoma.

— ◆ —

THE SOLAR ZENITH ANGLE

The skin makes vitamin D only when the sun is high enough in the sky, or at the proper solar zenith angle (altitude of the sun). When vitamin D–producing ultraviolet wavelengths arrive from the sun, they cannot penetrate the ozone, pollution, and clouds in the atmosphere unless they hit at or close to a right angle.

As a general rule, if your shadow is longer than you, you are not making as much vitamin D as you would if it were shorter. If your shadow is twice as long as you, you cannot make much vitamin D at all. If you live in the northern United States, in early morning, late evening, and sunny winter weather, your shadow is most likely more than twice as long as you—a sure sign that you are not making much vitamin D.

The wisest course is to make sure your child gets safe, short, and regular sun exposure during the warm months, recognizing that scientists and doctors don't know everything. In fact, they got us into this vitamin D deficiency epidemic in the first place.

Keep in mind that our ancestors evolved naked on the savannas of equatorial Africa, eating bugs and roots from the ground with the sun shining directly overhead. Humans have had a long evolutionary bond with the sun. Severing the relationship between your child and the sun is messing with Mother Nature—and she is a formidable opponent.

CHAPTER FIVE

VITAMIN D DEFICIENCY, AUTISM AND OTHER DISEASES: THE CONNECTION

I believe that the genetics of the vitamin D system and low vitamin D levels from lack of sunlight or supplementation conspire to prime the brain for autism. As you'll learn in this chapter, this interaction is not unique to autism, but it does explain why some children with low vitamin D levels get autism, while most do not.

THE VITAMIN D SYSTEM IS INHERITED

It makes sense that your vitamin D blood level depends entirely on how much sunlight you get or how much vitamin D you take. However, that is not true.[1] Up to 50 percent of your body's calcidiol blood levels are heritable, probably due to inherited differences in the enzymes that make calcidiol, such as 25-hydroxylase. Likewise, the amount of activated vitamin D your cells can make depends on the enzyme 1-hydroxylase, which is also inherited.[2] Your level of 24-hydroxylase (the enzyme that breaks down vitamin D in the body) is also inherited.[3] In this case, you do not want a lot. If you inherit lots of 24-hydroxylase, your vitamin D is constantly being broken down and destroyed before your body can use it.

You may inherit a few or many enzymes that metabolize vitamin D, with most of us having an average of both quantity and quality of all enzymes. One study of identical twins showed that, in boys, 86 percent of the variability in calcidiol level was attributable to genetic influence, but in females, only 17 percent was.[4] (That may explain the prevalence of autism in males.)

However, if you do have inherited deficiencies in your vitamin D enzyme system, you can counteract these tendencies by getting lots of sunshine or taking vitamin D in pill form. If you have an inherited deficiency in the vitamin D enzyme system, the amount of vitamin D you add from other sources becomes extremely important to your brain.

If your parents had adequate sun exposure before you were conceived, your mother sunbathed during pregnancy, or you were given adequate vitamin D supplements or allowed to be in the sun unprotected as an infant, chances are you have enough vitamin D—regardless of what vitamin D machinery you inherited. However, if the opposite happened and you have few sources of vitamin D and genetic deficiencies in vitamin D enzymes, your brain is in danger.

Inheritance is like a crapshoot. Some people are tall, and some are short; some get a little 24-hydroxylase, and some get a lot. Say you inherit a low number of vitamin D receptors and your parents don't put you in the sun without sunscreen. Your mother breastfeeds you but has low levels of vitamin D in her milk because she avoids the sun and does not supplement with vitamin D. She then weans you on pure fruit juice (no vitamin D) instead of vitamin D–enriched cow's milk. Also, more likely than not, you do not eat sardines, reindeer meat, or seagull eggs (all high in vitamin D).

By the time you are one year old, you have no source of vitamin D. Your low number of vitamin D receptors interacts with your low vitamin D level to injure your developing brain.

DID VITAMIN D CURE OUR SON?

Dr. Cannell:

My son has autism. When he was eight years old and weighed 64 pounds, we started him on 5,000 IU vitamin D daily (three capsules of BioTech Pharmacal's D$_3$Plus). It seemed to help, but there was much room for improvement. He was in special education in second grade and doing OK, but he had compulsive behaviors and difficult-to-control emotional outbursts.

In Minnesota, we get little to no sun exposure in winter, so we increased his dosage to four capsules per day (6,700 IU) when he turned nine and weighed 70 pounds.

After four weeks, his vitamin D level was 45 ng/mL [normal is 20–75 ng/mL]. His teachers noticed better memory, increased interaction with friends, and fewer problems focusing. He still was fidgety and hyperactive, but he had fewer outbursts.

We adjusted to five high-dose capsules of D$_3$Plus daily (8,300 IU). After two months, his vitamin D level was 72 ng/mL. His focus is much better, he has calmed down, and the emotional outbursts are gone. He is going to be mainstreamed in the third grade.

We no longer use speech or occupational therapies.

If I didn't know better, I'd say that vitamin D cured his autism.

Sincerely,

Ruby

Dear Ruby:

I am so glad for you and your family. However, make sure your son is under a physician's care. Just explain to the physician what you have done, the improvements you have seen, and that you want vitamin D levels in the high-normal range for your child. His vitamin D level, at 72 ng/mL, is just about right.

Ask his doctor to have his vitamin D levels tested every three or four months as long as he is taking five capsules of D$_3$Plus (8,300 IU) daily.

Vitamin D may help the core symptoms of autism, but it is highly unlikely that it cured it. At best, it helps control it. If he stopped taking vitamin D, his symptoms would return.

John Cannell, MD

In 2012, researchers discovered the same mechanism at work in heart disease—specifically in atherosclerosis, a buildup of cholesterol in the arteries that can lead to blockage.[5]

They measured the number of vitamin D receptors (inherited) in the arteries of a group of monkeys and then gave them small amounts of vitamin D. When they looked for atherosclerosis, they found it was much worse in the monkeys that had inherited low numbers of vitamin D receptors. That is, the low number of inherited receptors interacted with the small amount of vitamin D to produce atherosclerosis. The monkeys that inherited a higher number of receptors were able to tolerate the low amount of vitamin D without getting atherosclerosis.

I believe the genetics of autism interact with vitamin D in the environment in the same way.

◆

WHAT IS VITAMIN D DEFICIENCY?

Vitamin D deficiency depends on how you define it. According to most US laboratories, normal vitamin D levels range from 30 to 100 ng/mL. The lower limit is observed mostly in indoor workers, whose levels often fall below the natural range. Outdoor workers, such as lifeguards and roofers, have much higher levels (50–80 ng/mL). The only "normal" range that makes sense to me is the natural one we would have if we lived like our ancestors did.

Scientists tell us that humans lived for two million years naked under the equatorial sun. What were their vitamin D levels? Surely these levels, which most likely were close to those of modern-day lifeguards and roofers, are what they should be today. Therefore, we can use them as a guide to determine deficient levels.

One milligram (mg) of vitamin D is 40,000 IU. How much should adults take? The Vitamin D Council recommends a daily dose of 5,000 IU for healthy adults and 1,000 IU per 25 pounds for healthy children.

How do you know how much vitamin D is in a supplement? Deciphering labels on vitamin D supplements, or any supplement for that matter, can be an exercise in frustration. International unit (IU) is an ancient measurement used to specify a dose of vitamin D, but I often refer to a dose simply in terms of "units." Numbers of units can be confusing because 40,000 IU sounds like a large quantity, but 1 mg does not. These are, however, exactly the same dose: 40,000 IU equals 1 mg or 1,000 micrograms (mcg).

That means 5,000 IU/day is 125 mcg, which does not sound like a lot. In fact the correct dose of vitamin D (5,000–10,000 IU/day) is about the same as the correct dose of thyroid medication, 125–250 mcg per day.

CAUSE OR EFFECT?

Geneticists have been looking for mutations that cause autism. The actual DNA mutations are *not* the cause. The heritability of autism is due to the heritability of the vitamin D enzymatic system. The small de novo (new) point mutations in all 23 pairs of chromosomes of autistic children (but seldom in their parents) are *effects*, not causes, of autism. This is because vitamin D deficiency impairs the body's ability to repair DNA, the basis of our body's ability to fix mutations.

Vitamin D deficiency is a very new problem. The vitamin D system plus the lack of sun exposure has created a rapid and unfathomable new "genetic" epidemic. The genetics, however, lie in the inheritance of the vitamin D machinery—not in mutations.

MALE-TO-FEMALE RATIO IN AUTISM

The enzyme that activates vitamin D and its receptors in the body may be the primary culprit in the 5-to-1 male-female ratio in autism. Estrogen, a female hormone, makes activated vitamin D more potent.[6]

However, testosterone, a male hormone, appears not to have the same effect. The result: you have a new "genetic" disease that is much less common in girls than in boys.

SCOPE OF THE PROBLEM

Mounting evidence indicates that most people around the world are grossly vitamin D–deficient.[7] This should surprise no one, as modern men and women lead an indoor existence. Indoor lights, full-spectrum lights, bright lights, and sunlight coming through windows make no vitamin D. This is also true of the light boxes people use for seasonal affective disorder; they make no vitamin D. Sunlight striking skin that is covered in sunscreen makes no vitamin D at all if the sunscreen is applied correctly.[8]

> Scientists are discovering that vitamin D deficiency correlates with an astounding variety of diseases, such as cancer, heart disease, and multiple sclerosis.

The closest that most modern humans get to sun exposure is walking their dogs, picking up their mail, or walking through the parking lot to work. Moreover, these activities are typically done fully clothed, and clothes block almost 100 percent of vitamin D–producing ultraviolet B (UVB) radiation from sunlight.[8]

Scientists are discovering that vitamin D deficiency correlates with an astounding variety of diseases, such as cancer, heart disease, and multiple sclerosis.[9] That doesn't mean that vitamin D deficiency is the sole cause or that you won't get these diseases if you maintain proper levels of vitamin D; it just means that your risk of these diseases is probably low.

Vitamin D deficiency is widespread even in areas close to the equator. According to Michael Holick, vitamin D deficiency is an unrecognized global epidemic among children and adults.[9] *The New England Journal of Medicine* reported that, at one top US hospital, Massachusetts General Hospital in Boston, more than half of the inpatients were *severely* vitamin D–deficient.[10] According to the Endocrine Society, which is the world's largest association of endocrinologists (doctors who manage hormones), vitamin D levels of 40–60 ng/mL are ideal for otherwise healthy people.[15] Because the report from Massachusetts General Hospital defined deficiency as less than 15 ng/mL—not less than 40 ng/mL—the hospital's assessment was grossly underestimated. Based on 40 ng/mL, 95 percent of the hospital's patients were almost certainly severely deficient.

◆

NATURAL VERSUS NORMAL

Dutch researchers recently confirmed that modern-day hunter-gatherers in equatorial Africa have vitamin D levels of, on average, about 46 ng/mL, with levels as high as 105 ng/mL in one pregnant woman.[11,12] Research shows that virtually no one in the developed world has such levels, except outdoor workers and indoor workers who take at least 5,000 IU of vitamin D daily.

This study is both unique and critical because it defines "natural" versus "normal" vitamin D levels. Simple statistical averages and ranges of levels in modern humans, most of whom work inside and avoid the sun, determine normal levels. Levels such as those recently measured in Africa are natural and should be considered ideal unless and until we have good scientific evidence that they are harmful—and it is unlikely that nature would give us harmful vitamin D levels.

Some US studies have found that vitamin D deficiency is common in young adults (even in those who regularly drink vitamin D–fortified milk and take multivitamins), children, and even doctors in training.[13] In our most vulnerable populations (i.e., minorities, the elderly, and the chronically ill), it is nearly *universal*. Virtually all pregnant women in the United States are vitamin D–deficient because they avoid the sun and take prenatal vitamins that contain virtually meaningless quantities (600 IU) of vitamin D.[14] Four glasses of vitamin D–fortified milk (400 IU) will largely prevent the bone-softening disease rickets in toddlers (as long as adequate calcium is available), but adults would have to drink 50 8-ounce glasses of milk daily to get 5,000 IU. And drinking 50 glasses of fluid in a day could lead to death from fluid intoxication.

> Virtually all pregnant women in the United States are vitamin D-deficient because they avoid the sun and take prenatal vitamins that contain virtually meaningless quantities (600 IU) of vitamin D.[14]

The Vitamin D Council recommends levels of 50 ng/mL for healthy people. For those using vitamin D to manage a medical condition such as autism, the Vitamin D Council recommends levels in the high-normal range (70–80 ng/mL). A few labs list normal levels at 20–70 ng/mL based on a different laboratory technique; by these standards, autistic children should maintain levels of about 60 ng/mL. Until we know more, healthy people should maintain vitamin D levels of about 50 ng/mL, a level achieved by only a small fraction of people in the developed world.[15]

Over the past few years, as science has discovered that more diseases are associated with low vitamin D levels, US government estimates of what constitutes an ideal level have tripled. The higher that lower limit of "normal" goes, the more people fall into the deficient range.

Where do you fit?

If you are a young, healthy father-to-be and think you cannot be vitamin D–deficient, think again. If you're pregnant and believe you're not susceptible to vitamin D deficiency, think again. If you think your breastfeeding infant is getting everything he or she needs from your breast milk, think again. If you think your toddler is not vitamin D–deficient because he or she eats a good diet, think again. You may be in excellent health, eat a good diet, and take a multivitamin, yet you are still probably deficient—in the same manner that you might be iron- or magnesium-deficient.

What excites me—the reason I wrote this book, in fact—is that you may well reduce the risk that your child will have autism if your and your child's blood vitamin D levels are in the natural range. So, if someone asks you what percentage of the population is vitamin D–deficient, the correct answer is, "It depends on how you define it." However, even using the conservative cutoff of 30 ng/mL, most Americans are deficient, especially in winter in northern states.

BIOMARKERS

The definition of vitamin D deficiency also depends on which biomarker you use. A biomarker is the measure of a substance's effect on the body. It is an indicator of a biological state or condition. For example, say a vitamin D level of 40 ng/mL or higher effectively prevents influenza, but lower levels do not. We would then say that a calcidiol level of 40 ng/mL is a biomarker of an influenza effect. The most common biomarker for measuring vitamin D levels is parathyroid hormone (PTH). One of the many diseases vitamin D deficiency causes is secondary hyperparathyroidism, or elevated levels of PTH in the blood

caused by low vitamin D levels. As you might expect, because low vitamin D levels mean high PTH levels, high PTH levels are associated with
many illnesses. PTH levels do not decrease much after your vitamin D
level reaches 30 ng/mL, so a calcidiol level of 30 ng/mL is a biomarker for adequate parathyroid function.

> It takes very little vitamin D to prevent calcium deficiency and rickets, more to prevent excess PTH, and perhaps even more to prevent autism.

The problem with bio-
markers for vitamin D is that
they are different for differ-
ent conditions, as you would expect using the mountain pool metaphor.[16]
That is, it takes very little vitamin D to prevent calcium deficiency and
rickets, more to prevent excess PTH, and perhaps even more to prevent
autism. When there are limited reserves of vitamin D in the body, the
body must "decide" how to use them. The body knows that if vitamin D
levels become low enough (less than 5 ng/mL), blood calcium levels may
fall, resulting in death due to the heart's inability to contract. So when
vitamin D levels are low, the body does damage control: it stops using
vitamin D to prevent cancer and infections and uses it to preserve blood
calcium levels (i.e., to stay alive).

In my opinion, the best biomarker for vitamin D adequacy is an
evolutionary one. Scientists have long known that modern human
breast milk contains little or no vitamin D.[17] In medical school, I
always doubted that Paleolithic cavewomen exposed their newborns to the sun but rather hid them in caves for safety from preda-
tors. How could the perfect food not have vitamin D?

Bruce Hollis of the Medical University of South Carolina recently
answered this question when he asked, "What amount of vitamin D
is needed to transform human breast milk into an adequate source
of vitamin D?"[17] His answer shocked everyone: When breastfeeding

women take 6,000 IU of vitamin D daily (5,000 IU for themselves and 1,000 IU for their newborns), their breast milk is transformed into an adequate source of vitamin D. This means the reason breast milk contains no vitamin D is that almost all nursing mothers are deficient.[18] Vitamin D levels of 50 ng/mL in the mother ensure that breast milk is a rich source of vitamin D. Surely, this is the most important biomarker to date. We depend on it for survival.

Hollis also reported that in a study in which he gave breastfeeding women 2,000 or 4,000 IU daily and measured vitamin D levels in their suckling infants, he had to stop the study early because all the infants of the mothers receiving 2,000 IU were vitamin D–deficient. When the breastfeeding mothers took only 2,000 IU daily, their babies could not maintain adequate vitamin D levels.

What about American children? Are they deficient? To summarize one study, millions of US children 1–11 years old and nearly all black children may be vitamin D–deficient.[19] Scientists are only now beginning to understand the health consequences of such widespread deficiency in children.

Falling Vitamin D Levels

In 2011, scientists from the University of Colorado compared vitamin D levels in frozen blood samples from the late 1980s with blood from children in 2001.[19] The data showed a marked decrease in the more recent vitamin D levels. The same study showed that dramatic racial differences in vitamin D levels continue, with many blacks having extremely low levels. It is interesting to note that the study showed that many children had much lower vitamin D levels in 2001 than in 1988, before the epidemics of autism and vitamin D deficiency really began.

Conscious sun avoidance is not the only cause of this epidemic of childhood vitamin D deficiency. Video games have taken the place of outdoor games in many households.[20] Instead of playing hopscotch or baseball outside, most kids are inside a darkened room, building virtual worlds or killing aliens. We know that vitamin D levels in children fell at the same time the autism epidemic began. To my knowledge, no studies have examined vitamin D levels in pregnant women and future fathers over the same period, but if adult and child levels have fallen over the past 20 years, parents' vitamin D levels have probably fallen as well.

If the vitamin D theory of autism is valid, anything that increases the amount of vitamin D–producing ultraviolet light in the atmosphere should decrease the incidence of autism. For example, the disorder should be less common in sunny equatorial latitudes such as Somalia—at least they should have been before the modern era of sun avoidance. Studies from the early 1980s show that vitamin D levels vary by latitude (the closer you live to the Equator, the higher your level), but more recent studies show that vitamin D deficiency is common in almost every country in the world, except for developing nations close to the Equator—that is, areas where people wear fewer clothes and don't use sunscreen.

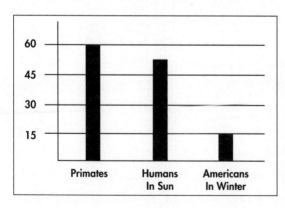

This graphic representation of vitamin D nutritional status through the ages indicates that 40–60 ng/mL appears to be optimal.

In fact, William Grant recently published a paper that studied the association of vitamin D–producing UV radiation in sunshine and the prevalence of autism in the United States.[21] In his paper, Grant found that the prevalence of autism was as many as three times higher in states with the least UV radiation.

SHOW ME THE PROOF

I've established that the autism epidemic arrived at about the same time vitamin D deficiency became widespread. In my first paper on autism and vitamin D, I outlined all the evidence I could find that parental or early-childhood vitamin D deficiency is the primary cause of autism.[20]

As I referenced in that paper, John McGrath and colleagues in Australia and others have repeatedly demonstrated that vitamin D deficiency causes brain dysfunction.[20] Recently, impaired child language development was associated with low maternal vitamin D levels.[22] Even more recently, Christopher Gillberg and colleagues of the Gillberg Neuropsychiatric Institute in Sweden reviewed 35 papers on vitamin D and autism and concluded that there is an "urgent" need for research in this area.[23]

VITAMIN D DEFICIENCY AND OTHER DISEASES

Over the past few years, scientists have discovered that a staggering number of diseases are associated to some degree with low levels of vitamin D.[24,25] The list includes so many illnesses that some health professionals consider the health claims for vitamin D to be outlandish. Many don't read the research or simply dismiss vitamin D as an overhyped and impossible cure-all. They cannot fathom that low levels of a common, well-known, and inexpensive vitamin are associated with higher incidences of most varieties of internal cancers, heart disease, diabetes, depression, multiple sclerosis, chronic pain, lung disease, hip fractures, arthritis, and even obesity.[24,25] Such doubters simply do not understand how activated vitamin D works; it is a steroid hormone that turns genes on or off.

Vitamin D may even help prevent and treat influenza.[26–28] Like autism, influenza has many vitamin D risk factors, such as being at its worst when the amount of sunlight is low (winter), being worse in cities where vitamin D levels are low due to tall buildings, and being more severe and common among blacks. Evidence indicates that vitamin D dramatically increases the number of antibiotic peptides, naturally occurring antibiotics in the lungs, respiratory tract, immune cells, intestines, and skin.

> Vitamin D may even help prevent and treat influenza.

Cathelicidin is one of these naturally occurring peptides. It rapidly kills harmful viruses, bacteria, and fungi by destroying their outer coats. (One of the most common complaints from mothers of autistic children is that they are often sick; infections should lessen with vitamin D.) John White's group at McGill University in Quebec, Canada, was among the first to show how robustly vitamin D increases production of antimicrobial peptides.[29]

When I felt comfortable we'd worked out the relationship between influenza and vitamin D, my colleagues and I published two papers.[26,27] We presented evidence that vitamin D levels have been falling over the past 30 years. We also cited several large studies showing that both hospitalizations for and deaths from influenza in the elderly have increased over the same period, despite dramatically increasing influenza immunization rates in the elderly.[30,31]

Randomized controlled trials show that influenza immunizations are helpful. So immunizations should have reduced both hospitalization and death rates in the elderly, but they haven't. Influenza immunization rates in the elderly went from about 20 percent in 1980 to about 85 percent in 2010, but deaths and hospitalizations from influenza continued to increase. We explained that increasing immunization rates could not counteract falling vitamin D levels' adverse effect on the immune system.

Several months after we published our first paper, the results of a randomized controlled interventional trial (the gold standard of research) confirmed our theory: even 2,000 units (50 mcg) of vitamin D daily reduced respiratory infections in adults.[32] As of this writing, we don't know how many respiratory viruses are sensitive to the antimicrobial peptides that vitamin D increases. What we do think is that a family taking adequate doses of vitamin D has fewer and less severe colds and influenza. A recent review and meta-analysis concluded that vitamin D helps prevent respiratory tract infections.[33]

A recent study in *The Journal of the American Medical Association* found that vitamin D had no effect on colds and flu.[34] However, this study used huge monthly doses of vitamin D rather than daily doses, and it did not compare the vitamin D treatment group with a vitamin D–deficient control group. The researchers cited three positive studies of vitamin D and influenza that used daily doses of vitamin D and acknowledged that large monthly doses might not work.

Since I proposed the theory that vitamin D helps fight infections such as influenza, dozens of studies have supported the theory.[33] It took six years for this to happen. The autism theory has one crucial characteristic of a good theory: it can easily be proven wrong. A study of the effect of high-dose daily vitamin D on autism symptoms in children would be inexpensive and simple.

One such study is in progress at the University of California–San Francisco, financed by the Vitamin D Council.[35] Another exciting study was recently completed but was not yet published at the time of this writing. It showed that 5,000 IU/day improved symptoms in 80 percent of children with autism.[36]

IN CONCLUSION

Although it's a plausible theory, there is no incontrovertible proof that vitamin D deficiency contributes to autism. So if you're pregnant, should you take vitamin D, go out in the sun, or wait for more science? If you have an autistic child, should you give him a vitamin D supplement and have him play in the sun without sunscreen, or should you wait for more science?

In other words, should you let your child have both autism and probable vitamin D deficiency until science completes its work? I can't tell you what to do, but I do know what I'd do if I had an autistic child or if I were advising parents-to-be or a pregnant woman.

I arrived at my conclusion using a simple risk-benefit analysis. What is the risk of having high-normal vitamin D levels, the levels lifeguards have in summer? What are the potential benefits? Studies suggest that the benefits of higher vitamin D levels are enormous, while the risk is almost non-existent.

CHAPTER SIX

VITAMIN D, AUTISM AND SKIN COLOR

I n the United States, people with a lot of melanin (dark pigment) in their skin tend to have low levels of vitamin D. Some black women of childbearing age have extremely low or virtually no detectable vitamin D in their blood, and their fetuses develop in an extremely vitamin D–poor environment. According to the CDC, autism spectrum disorder is no more common among blacks than whites.[1] However, numerous studies contradict those findings.

Such studies are difficult to conduct because they raise sensitive social and racial issues, although three of four US population studies found that autism is more common in black children than in white children—sometimes appreciably so.[2-5] The latest population-based study, from the University of California at Los Angeles, published in July 2014 in *Pediatrics*, found that autism (especially autism with mental impairment) is more common in blacks.[6]

Also, at least one scientist, Bruce Ames, of the University of California, Berkeley, writes that the CDC did not adjust for socioeconomic factors in its analysis of skin color and autism rates.[7] According to Patrick and Ames, once corrected for socioeconomic status, the rate of autism is higher in blacks and the risk for autism in individuals with higher socioeconomic status is twice as high in blacks than in whites.

Furthermore, in Europe, autism rates are higher in children of dark-skinned immigrants.[8] In fact, studies have consistently found that dark-skinned immigrants are more likely to give birth to autistic children than are native light-skinned women.[9–11] M. Barnevik-Olsson and colleagues found that children of Somali background had four times the rate of autism than did children of non-Somali origin living in Sweden.[11] In addition, the researchers found that the age at which the developmental deviation was noted in Somali children was younger and that the children's definite intellectual impairment was more severe. In other words, autism was more common and severe in dark-skinned children.

Other studies have reported the higher risk of autism in dark-skinned immigrants. A population study in a small part of Sweden identified 45 children 13 and younger diagnosed with autism.[12] Fifteen of these children (27 percent) were born to parents who had migrated to Sweden. The author of that study, Gillberg, found a much higher rate of autism in immigrants than in native Swedish parents and had no explanation for it. In 1995, Gillberg reported that 15 percent of children born to Ugandan mothers in Sweden had autism; that's nearly 200 times higher than the rate of the general population of Swedish children.[13] Gillberg could not explain this dramatic difference, but the vitamin D theory explains it perfectly.

In 2010, D. V. Keen and colleagues found that black women born outside the United Kingdom had a significantly higher risk of having a child with ASD than black women born in the United Kingdom, with the highest risk observed for Caribbean-born mothers.[10] In fact, black mothers had an eightfold higher risk of having an autistic child than white mothers.

In 2008, Elizabeth Gorman, a reporter for the *StarTribune*, noted that many special education students in Minneapolis public schools are Somali.[14] "We're definitely seeing it, and something is triggering it," said Chris Bentley, director of a nonprofit in Minneapolis that assists autistic children. "This is a much bigger issue than we thought," he said, adding that it may lead to clues about the causes of autism.

David Kirby of *The Huffington Post* wrote that 6 percent of the Minneapolis school district's enrollment is Somali.[15] However, more than 17 percent of students in the district's early childhood special education autism program are Somali. He added that almost one-fourth of all autistic children in the district's low-functioning classrooms are Somali.

M. J. Dealberto discovered that dark-skinned immigrants in the United States and Europe are especially likely to give birth to children with autism.[10] The elevated risk was highly significant when she used a strict definition of autistic disorders as opposed to a looser definition of pervasive developmental disorder.

The CDC found higher rates of mild intellectual disability in blacks than in whites.[16] I believe the CDC has not found a higher rate of autism among blacks because the agency failed to include some children with severe autism with intellectual disability. As mentioned above, the CDC reported that black children have significantly higher rates of mild intellectual disability than white children, and socioeconomic factors cannot explain all the differences.[16] Because severe autism is usually associated with intellectual disability, it seems likely that undersampling black children with autism and intellectual disability, together with the failure to correct for socioeconomic status, may explain the CDC's negative findings because so many other studies find that autism is more common among people with dark skin.

BLACK WOMEN AND MOTHERS OF AUTISTIC CHILDREN

If the vitamin D theory is true, similar pregnancy complications should be common to both black women and mothers of autistic children. Compared with pregnant white women, pregnant black women have a higher likelihood of early labor, cesarean births, bleeding, high blood pressure, diabetes, and infants who are small for gestational age and have low Apgar scores.[17] Mothers of children later diagnosed with autism show a similar pattern of complications.[18] (Healthcare professionals perform the Apgar test on newborns to assess breathing effort, heart rate, muscle tone, reflexes, and skin color.)

One study showed that the risk of autism was associated with being small for gestational age and having low Apgar scores.[19] Another showed that, during the prenatal (before birth) and neonatal (shortly after birth) periods, the risk factors for ASD included preterm birth, cesarean birth, low Apgar scores, and being small for gestational age.[20] Metabolic complications, such as maternal diabetes, hypertension, and obesity, all increase the risk of the baby eventually having autism.[21] Black mothers often have similar metabolic complications.[22] Thus the birth and delivery complications of black women and mothers of autistic children are similar, as would be expected if blacks were more likely to have autism.[22–24]

SEVERE VITAMIN D DEFICIENCY

In 2002, the CDC reported that severe vitamin D deficiency is 24 times more common among young black women than among young white women. Shanna Nesby-O'Dell and colleagues found that almost half of young black women had levels lower than 15 ng/mL.[25] Most disturbing, 12 percent had levels lower than 10 ng/mL, compared with only 0.5 percent of white women.

More recent studies of vitamin D deficiency during pregnancy show striking racial disparities in maternal vitamin D levels. L. M. Bodnar and colleagues of the University of Pennsylvania found that only 4 percent of black women and 30 percent of white women in the northern United States were vitamin D–sufficient during early pregnancy.[26] That is, 96 percent of pregnant black women did not have adequate vitamin D levels. Their infants fared little better.

Furthermore, 45 percent of the pregnant black women—but only 2 percent of the pregnant white women—were very seriously deficient, with vitamin D levels below 10 ng/mL. Prenatal vitamins containing the usual 400 units of vitamin D offered little protection for mothers and infants. Ninety percent of the women in this study reported taking such prenatal vitamins.

Vitamin D deficiency discriminates based on the amount of melanin, a very proficient and ever-present sunscreen. The more melanin in your skin, the longer it takes to make vitamin D in your skin and build up optimal levels.

◆

MELANIN AND VITAMIN D ABSORPTION

If vitamin D is so important, why did early Africans evolve to have skin that inhibits them from quickly absorbing vitamin D? Our ancestors in equatorial Africa had more than enough sunlight. What they needed was a way to protect against sunburn. Dark skin also protects the body's folic acid, which is stored in the skin and can be destroyed by sunlight.

Studies show that black people can produce as much vitamin D as people with lighter skin. It just takes longer. Due to dark skin pigment that blocks ultraviolet ray absorption, blacks need up to 10 times longer in the sun than whites to produce the same amount of vitamin D—a level they would have gotten in Paleolithic Africa. Black skin is perfectly designed for tropical latitudes, as melanin protects the folic acid stores deep in the skin, and abundant sun exposure ensures adequate vitamin D status.

Humans evolving in Africa a million years ago had plenty of vitamin D despite their dark skin, as do hunter-gatherers who live there today. Modern-day hunter-gatherers in equatorial Africa have natural blood levels (an average of 46 ng/mL) of vitamin D. In fact, one of the highest vitamin D blood levels from sunshine alone that was ever recorded, 105 ng/mL, was in a pregnant woman in modern-day equatorial Africa.[27]

BLACKS AND DISEASE

According to the National Center for Health Statistics, the life expectancy for a black male born in 2004 is 69.5 years, versus 75.7 years for a white male born the same year.[31] What makes blacks more likely to die young than whites? Why the racial disparity?

In general, blacks die younger than whites due to a bewildering and seemingly disconnected array of diseases. Even ailments that are less common among blacks, such as breast cancer, are deadlier than they are in their white counterparts. Is this entirely due to differences in factors such as income, neighborhood status, ability to buy nutritious food, educational level, and housing? Or could a near-universal health difference in blacks be causing the higher death rate? Is there a single substance involved in all the diseases that prematurely kill blacks?

Since 2000, a number of studies have documented dramatic differences in blood levels of vitamin D according to skin color. These studies, when considered with clinical studies of vitamin D deficiency, offer scientists and physicians a unique chance to erase some health inequities that burden blacks. Opportunities like this are rare, but government officials, private citizens, and the press must learn about the findings before they can take action.[28,29]

OUR SON IS THRIVING WITH VITAMIN D

Dear Dr. Cannell:

I have a four-year-old high-functioning autistic son who could be the "poster child" for the vitamin D theory of autism. During our dark Idaho winters, he would fall apart: flapping, anxiety, toe walking, sleeplessness, repetitive questions, fixations, social avoidance, lack of eye contact, inability to concentrate, hyperactivity, and staring spells. In the winter, he went to classes with severely autistic children and fit right in. In the summer, he did so well that he was released from occupational, physical, speech, and behavioral therapy.

Our son weighed 38 pounds when we started giving him 2,000 IU of vitamin D daily and then increased it to 5,000 IU. His vitamin D level had climbed from 39 to 84 ng/mL. He was doing so much better, even going into winter. Our pediatrician advised us to reduce his vitamin D dosage to 1,500 IU daily; however, at this dosage, symptoms began to resurface. Our pediatrician then increased his dosage to 4,000 IU daily and will check his vitamin D level every few months.

Marsha

Dear Marsha:

I am glad your son is improving. If his vitamin D level were to rise to 150–200 ng/mL (which would require about 15,000–20,000 IU daily), the worst that could happen would be a mild elevation in his blood calcium, which would normalize when the dose was reduced.

Vitamin D toxicity can occur, but only if vitamin D levels remain above 200 ng/mL for years without detection. That's why regular blood tests are needed when children are on adult doses of vitamin D.

Finally, I am glad that your son's doctor is open-minded. Most doctors are doing what they have been trained to do, which includes recommending no more than 400 IU daily in children. However, when they see the dramatic improvement, some are willing to try higher vitamin D levels.

John Cannell, MD

HOW MUCH HAVE YOU LEARNED?

The following questions will help you digest the information in this chapter. How many can you answer correctly?

1. Fatal cancers are much more common in blacks than in whites, and low vitamin D levels are associated with fatal cancers. True or false?

    True.[30–32] Black men have a 40 percent higher death rate from all cancers combined than whites; for black women, the rate is 20 percent higher. Furthermore, low vitamin D levels are a risk factor for virtually all fatal cancers.[33]

2. Heart disease is more common in black than in white Americans, and low vitamin D levels are associated with heart attacks. True or false?

    True.[34] Blacks have the highest overall heart disease mortality rate and the highest rate of sudden death of any US ethnic group—particularly at younger ages. Coincidentally, patients with low vitamin D levels have twice the risk of heart attack as those with the highest levels.[35]

3. Blacks are at high risk for strokes, and low vitamin D levels are associated with strokes. True or false?

    True.[36] Blacks have more strokes than whites, especially when they are young. Furthermore, a study found low vitamin D blood levels in most patients with acute stroke; it provided evidence that low levels preceded the stroke.[37]

4. High blood pressure is more common in black than in white Americans, and low vitamin D levels predict who will develop hypertension. True or false?

True. High blood pressure is more common and severe in populations of African descendants living outside Africa than in any other population.[38] A Harvard study found that men with the lowest vitamin D levels were six times more likely to have high blood pressure and that women with the lowest levels were three times more likely to have high blood pressure than those with the highest levels.[39]

5. Diabetes is more common in blacks than whites, and diabetes is associated with low vitamin D levels. True or false?
   True. Type 2 diabetes and its complications are disproportionately more common in blacks than in other groups.[40] Not surprisingly, the association between vitamin D levels and blood sugar is strong. Poor diabetes control and low vitamin D levels are also strongly associated.[41]

6. Kidney failure is more common in blacks than in whites, and low vitamin D levels are the rule among people with kidney disease. True or false?
   True. Blacks shoulder a disproportionately high burden of kidney disease compared with whites.[42] Patients with kidney failure on dialysis are much more likely to be vitamin D–deficient, and low vitamin D levels precede dialysis. That is, patients with kidney disease have low vitamin D levels before they start dialysis.[43, 44]

7. Multiple sclerosis (MS) is more common, severe, and prolonged in blacks than in whites, and low vitamin D levels are associated with multiple sclerosis. True or false?

True. Blacks are more likely to develop MS at a younger age, have greater disability from it, and experience longer disease duration than whites.[45] A Harvard study found that those with the lowest vitamin D levels were about three times more likely to have MS than those with high levels. However, the vitamin D levels of blacks were so low that researchers were unable to accurately determine the association.[46]

8. Conditions such as the autoimmune disease rheumatoid arthritis are more common in blacks than in whites, and low vitamin D levels are common in those with rheumatic conditions. True or false?
    True. Deaths from aggressive rheumatic conditions are higher in black than in white Americans.[47] A 2014 study found significantly lower vitamin D levels in rheumatoid arthritis patients, and calcidiol levels were correlated with severity of disease.[48]

9. Pneumonia and flu deaths are more common in blacks than in whites, and vitamin D prevents respiratory infections. True or false?
    True. The death rate from pneumonia and influenza is higher in blacks than in whites, with black infants twice as likely to die from pneumonia.[49] Results from double-blind, placebo-controlled trials showed that vitamin D prevents influenza.[50]

10. Gum (periodontal) disease, which is associated with low vitamin D levels, is more common in blacks than whites. True or false?
    True. Gum disease is more common in blacks than in whites.[51] A study found that vitamin D levels were significantly and inversely associated with gum disease.[52]

CHAPTER SEVEN

YOUR SKIN IS A VITAMIN D MACHINE: YOU'RE THE DRIVER

Two facts I learned about vitamin D changed my life. Maybe they'll change yours and your child's, too.

1. You make incredible amounts of vitamin D from the sun very quickly.

2. The level of activated vitamin D in your body's tissues depends largely on your behavior.[1]

In just 30 minutes, a sunbather easily makes more than 10 times the amount of vitamin D than the government's Institute of Medicine says you need all day.[2] This tells us two very important things about vitamin D: (1) The 10,000 units the skin produces in 30 minutes make the 100 units in a glass of milk seem irrelevant. For people with fair skin, production of 10,000 units happens within minutes of full-body sun exposure; and (2) People who take 10,000 units of vitamin D per day are not at risk for vitamin D poisoning. In fact, no adult has *ever* been reported to have overdosed after taking even 20,000 units per day, and no one has ever reported vitamin D poisoning from too much sun exposure. Therefore, 10,000 units per day is not toxic.

For kids, you can count the number of cases of vitamin D toxicity reported in the medical literature in the past 30 years on just one hand. Even these cases are dosage errors, such as giving an entire dropper full instead of a drop. Furthermore, these few cases resulted in only high blood calcium levels, not death. To the best of my knowledge, the most recent childhood deaths from vitamin D toxicity were reported in England in the late 1940s, again due to major dosage errors. In contrast, more than 100 infants die every year in the United States from over-the-counter cough and cold medicine.[3]

◆

VITAMIN D HYPERSENSITIVITY

Some people are quite sensitive to vitamin D. About .02 percent of the US population has sarcoidosis, a disease of inflammatory growths inside the body. After visiting the beach or taking even a small dose of vitamin D, people with sarcoidosis may have high blood calcium levels that cause heart irregularities. People with sarcoidosis, certain other related diseases, and a few rare cancers may have high blood calcium with small amounts of vitamin D. However, this type of vitamin D hypersensitivity is unusual, very rare in children, and very different from vitamin D poisoning.

OUR "MANUFACTURE" LEVELS

That first fact also tells you that the upper limit for adults (4,000 units per day) from the Institute of Medicine's Food and Nutrition Board is simply wrong.[4] A light-skinned person produces that much after only 10 minutes of full-body sunbathing. It's increasingly apparent that the US government made a *huge* mistake with vitamin D, one that may dwarf virtually all previous nutrition-related errors.

Through the Food and Nutrition Board, the government told us that adequate daily intake (as opposed to the upper limit) of vitamin D is only 400–800 units per day, depending on age.[4] It now appears that most adults need about 5,000 units per day to obtain natural (50 ng/mL) vitamin D levels. That recommendation was off by a factor of 10.

Why do humans make such large amounts of vitamin D when we go into the sun, and why do we make it so quickly? The next question is, Would nature have produced a system as complicated as our vitamin D machinery if it were unimportant to health? From what I know of biology, the answer to this last question is no. Nor would the skin make vitamin D so quickly if it were unimportant.

The substance is so important that the body evolved a system to take advantage of even short periods of sun exposure. But why? We are just beginning to find out. It is beginning to look as if vitamin D is one of the most important linchpins of good health. It is a "repair and maintenance" steroid hormone. Whether we have infection, heart disease, or cancer, vitamin D appears to take steps to limit or repair that damage.[5] Vitamin D works at the level of the human genome, turning genes on and off at a dizzying rate.[6]

Is this the beginning of the vitamin D era, or is it another vitamin error?[7] Errors concerning vitamins have happened before, such as studies that revealed the unsuspected toxicity of vitamin A or the ineffectiveness of vitamin E. In these cases, widespread claims for good health *preceded* carefully conducted science and led to the scientific downfall of both vitamins.

However, if you choose to just wait and see, you still must choose which vitamin D level to wait with—a natural one or a normal one. The conservative approach is to maintain natural levels while you wait for science to do its work.

VITAMIN D HAS RESTORED OUR HOPE

Dear Dr. Cannell:

I have been giving my six-year-old son and eight-year-old daughter vitamin D supplements. The biggest changes have been improved awareness, reduced hyperactivity, and a small increase in speech and language in my son.

My daughter, who has moderate autism, has begun to improve. About two months after we started the vitamin D, she pointed to the TV and said, "Mom, what's that?" I was stunned for several reasons: (1) she never refers to me by name or attempts to get my attention in that way; (2) she had never before asked me what an object was; and (3) she never spontaneously points at objects.

I can say with certainty that that was truly the beginning of her use of spontaneous language. She was somewhat verbal before the vitamin D, but typically she communicated only her wants and needs.

My son, who has moderate autism with possible attention-deficit hyperactivity disorder, is showing dramatic improvement. He is answering yes/no questions with accuracy. He can choose between two options when presented. He refers to others by name.

Although we still have a way to go with each child, when I look at their faces, it is almost as though a switch has been turned on in their brains.

I want to also mention that the dosage I had been giving the kids was 10,000 IU/day. Now we are down to 7,000 IU/day, and their vitamin D levels are OK. I have hope now, and I can't tell you what it was like living with no hope.

Thanks. Mary

Dear Mary:

I am so happy for you. Your doctor must keep checking your kids' vitamin D levels on 7,000 IU of vitamin D daily and keep their levels at about 80 ng/mL, if the lab's reference range is 30–100 ng/mL. I am so glad it seemed to help; it is why I went to medical school.

John Cannell, MD

Our "Activated" Levels

That second amazing fact is that levels of activated vitamin D depend almost entirely on human behavior—whether you stay inside or go outside, and whether you take a vitamin D supplement.

Activated vitamin D is the key. It can unlock as many as 2,000 human vitamin D–responsive genes, which is 5 percent of the active human genome.[8-10] If you're not getting sunshine or taking a supplement, you are vitamin D–deficient—no exceptions. Vitamin D is the only vitamin for which you cannot achieve natural blood levels through diet. It's that simple.

> If you're not getting sunshine or taking a supplement, you are vitamin D–deficient—no exceptions.

The only other sources of vitamin D in food are wild cold-water fatty fish such as salmon and sardines, seagull eggs, reindeer meat, and mushrooms dried with their gills toward the sun. You cannot get enough vitamin D from diet alone unless you eat these foods daily and in abundance. Nature meant for the body to make vitamin D in the skin and for food to be a minor supplement.

Concerns for Toddlers

Low levels of vitamin D appear to be damaging the genome of men before they father children, of pregnant women, and of young children, especially toddlers, as their brains grow.

Toddlers who are kept out of the sun or slathered in sunscreen may lose their primary source of vitamin D when their mothers wean them from formula to juice.[11] (Most breast-fed babies also get some vitamin D–rich formula toward the end of breastfeeding.)

Thirty years ago in the United States, mothers weaned toddlers to cow's milk, which contains vitamin D. The 100 units of vitamin D in a glass of milk is not much for an adult but is an appreciable quantity for a 20-pound child. (The government added vitamin D to cow's milk in the 1950s to prevent rickets in children.)

In 2006, R. B. Walker and colleagues reported that only 14 percent of mothers thought cow's milk was the best drink for weaned infants; most women (84 percent) viewed fruit juice, which seldom contains vitamin D, as most suitable.[11]

Infant Supplements

In 2010, *Pediatrics,* the most respected medical journal in the world for pediatricians, published a frightening study from the CDC.[12] The authors found that the use of oral vitamin D supplements in infants was very low and not meeting the recommendations of the American Academy of Pediatrics (AAP). The percentage of infants meeting AAP intake recommendations (400 units/day) was only 1–13 percent, varying by age.

Among infants who consumed breast milk but no formula, only 5 percent met recommended AAP intakes. Among mixed-fed infants, only 14 percent met the AAP recommendations. Among infants who consumed formula with no breast milk, only 37 percent met the AAP recommendations.

Sun Protection

In 2001, the CDC reported that sun protection for our children was *"almost complete,"*[13] meaning that children were now being protected from the sun with sunscreen, clothes, or sun avoidance. The change in feeding habits and, more important, the prolific use of sunscreen, have combined to rob our toddlers of their two best sources of vitamin D: sunshine and vitamin D–fortified cow's milk. Scientists know that the body cannot make activated vitamin D on its own without the building blocks supplied by the skin and the sun or supplements.[14]

In Conclusion

Perhaps the reason vitamin D levels depend on human behavior is that nature never conceived of the possibility that doctors, the government, video games, computers, and cosmetic and sunscreen firms could so easily get us out of the sun. After all, we had been in the sun for more than two million years. Why would we up and leave it one day in the 1980s?

If you are old enough, you probably slip on occasion and use the term *suntan lotion* instead of *sunscreen*. You also probably remember that, in 1975, drugstores sold coconut butter and baby oil for a trip to the beach; by 1985, the same store was selling sun protection factor (SPF) 20. Now the common SPF is 100, and just try to get coconut butter for sunbathing.

Taking leave of the sun is highly unnatural. Do you remember how good sunshine feels in the springtime, how you crave it in the winter? Studies show that sunlight produces endorphins, the same calming molecule made after vigorous exercise. Perhaps it's because nature wants to reward us when we do something good for our bodies, such as exercising or sunbathing.

In the larger picture, the one in evolutionary time, our journey out of the sun, as far as nature is concerned, is meaningless. Nature will deal with it, I suspect, by eventually mutating a gene allowing the building blocks of vitamin D to be made inside the body. Remember, nature works by natural selection, killing those without the necessary genetic adaptation and favoring those with it. It is a brutal process. Until then, vitamin D building blocks must be supplied by humans via a supplement or ultraviolet light such as sunlight. The decision is yours.

CHAPTER EIGHT

How Does Vitamin D Work in Autism?

We know that vitamin D may improve autism symptoms, but how? Nine possible mechanisms increase when an autistic child starts getting enough vitamin D. I believe a combination of them is at work in treating autism.

1. DNA Repair

Autism may be a genetic disease that isn't inherited.[1] But how can that be? It appears that many small, new, genetic mutations such as those seen in autism occur either in the womb or during early childhood.[2] These mutations are the most common genetic findings in autistic children. Scientists have identified at least five vitamin D–dependent genes that direct DNA repair proteins. These proteins have only one job: to fix your broken DNA.

James Fleet of Purdue University and colleagues wrote an excellent article on how vitamin D helps prevent cancer, and he almost offhandedly mentioned DNA repair as one of vitamin D's mechanisms of action in cancer.[3] Likewise, H. D. Halicka and colleagues wrote that vitamin D is responsible for protecting the genome from genetic damage.[4] Repairing the genome is just another one of vitamin D's repair and maintenance functions. Once your body has enough vitamin D, including enough to overcome any inherited defect of the vitamin D system, all those little genetic repair train cars can chug happily along, fixing the multiple small genetic variations.

On occasion, humans have major problems with their DNA called double-stranded breaks. Instead of just one strand of the DNA breaking in response to damaging environmental oxidants, poisons, radiation, or other DNA enemies, both DNA strands break, and we are in big trouble. Those cells can easily go on to become cancerous. According to H. J. Ting and colleagues, activated vitamin D protects cells by producing DNA repair genes that fix these double-stranded breaks.[5] The authors' findings also suggest that vitamin D guards the genome by controlling DNA repair. If this is true, vitamin D can help repair DNA.

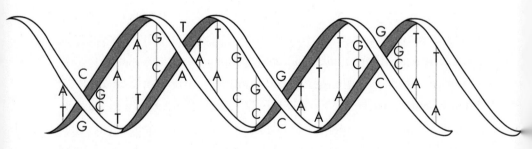

DNA is a double-stranded molecule held together by weak bonds between four components: adenine (A), cytosine (C), guanine (G), and thymine (T). Researchers think vitamin D is an important factor in repairing DNA bond breaks, a cause of mutations.

2. DNA PROTECTION

DNA protection is different from DNA repair in that preventing DNA damage is preferable to repairing the damage once it has occurred. In 2001, M. Chatterjee reported that vitamin D stabilizes chromosomal structure and prevents DNA double-stranded breaks.[6] She concluded that the role of vitamin D in repairing gene mutation and DNA strand breaks is much more important than we originally thought. Because some scientists think that vitamin D helps repair DNA, it's not outlandish to think that vitamin D has a role in protecting DNA as well.

Three scientists from the University of Sydney Medical School in Australia recently reviewed test-tube, animal, and human studies in detail, concluding that vitamin D does appear to protect DNA

> The role of vitamin D in repairing gene mutation and DNA strand breaks is much more important than we originally thought.

from mutations.[7] They went so far as to say that vitamin D deficiency is associated with DNA damage from various cellular stresses and that obtaining adequate vitamin D is important in preventing DNA damage.

This research supports my theory that the widespread different tiny mutations and DNA damage in autism are the effects of a genetically impaired vitamin D system interacting with inadequate amounts of vitamin D building blocks. This interaction causes DNA injury not to be repaired. DNA differences have confused geneticists for years because they assumed that any genetic abnormality in autism was a cause rather than an effect.

IT'S ALMOST AS IF HE WERE CURED

Dear Dr. Cannell:

I am writing because I believe my seven-year-old autistic son is strongly affected by vitamin D. We live in the northeast, and he spends lots of time outside in the summer, and I usually forget to put sunscreen on him. Every year, he has the same patterns of behavior and ability. Every July, he begins feeling much better, seems to be comfortable in his skin, does not have as much self-stimulatory behavior, can eat a variety of foods, and has language (this past summer, he was using 14-word sentences). By November, he can't even ask for juice. He becomes more exclusive and emotional, has tantrums, and is easily frustrated.

His vitamin D level in April was 25 ng/mL. I started giving him 5,000 IU of vitamin D daily, and after three weeks, he told me to "turn off the TV" and "clean up the water." And he was OK with being in another room or outside alone (he is usually afraid to be alone).

After six weeks, we had continued success with language, and he starting going to the bathroom by himself. We took him to see his pediatrician, and she insisted we reduce his vitamin D from 5,000 to 1,000 IU daily. In three weeks, his language abilities began to deteriorate.

His doctor reluctantly agreed to put him back on 5,000 IU/day if we got regular blood tests. Within a month, he was using his muscles more and fully lifting and bending his legs on the swing outside. After 6 weeks, his blood level was 66 ng/mL. His improvements continue in language and emotional connection, and he has few tantrums or obsessive behavior.

It's almost as if he were cured.

Jane

Dear Jane:

It is too early to say that vitamin D cured your son's autism. However, a simple risk/benefit analysis suggests that children with autism should be diagnosed and aggressively treated for vitamin D deficiency.

John Cannell, MD

3. ANTI-INFLAMMATORY ACTIONS

Autism is a disease of inflammation.[8] According to X. Guillot and colleagues, no substance is quite as anti-inflammatory as vitamin D because it makes the immune system "smarter."[9] Activated vitamin D in particular has well-known direct and indirect anti-inflammatory effects.

Vitamin D is an immune modulator that reduces inflammation while enhancing protective immune responses. Many immune cells release the enzyme that activates vitamin D, arming the immune system with a potent anti-inflammatory weapon. This may be the second reason that high doses of vitamin D are needed in autistic children (the first being to overcome their genetic tendency toward an ineffective vitamin D system). Studies show that molecules called cytokines, which promote inflammation, are consistently elevated in autistic children. Numerous randomized controlled trials have shown that vitamin D reduces the number of inflammatory cytokines.[10–16]

> Recent research reveals that activated vitamin D has multiple anti-inflammatory effects.

Recent research reveals that activated vitamin D has multiple anti-inflammatory effects.[17] First, it inhibits the production and biological actions of prostaglandins, which promote inflammation and are elevated in autism.[18] Second, vitamin D inhibits a substance called nuclear factor-kappa B, which promotes inflammation and is involved in signaling between neurons in the brains of people with autism.[19]

These anti-inflammatory effects of vitamin D may explain the reported associations between vitamin D and a large number of inflammatory diseases, including autoimmune disorders such as rheumatoid arthritis and lupus.[20] In lab animals and humans, some studies show vitamin D helps inflammatory diseases.[21] Thus, vitamin D is a key prospect for the treatment of diseases with autoimmune aspects, such as autism.

4. ANTIBODY MANUFACTURE

In more than 160 human autoimmune diseases, the body makes antibodies that attack its own tissues. These diseases include type 1 diabetes (insulin-dependent diabetes), Lou Gehrig's disease (also known as ALS), and lupus. They arise from an improper immune response to substances and tissues normally present in the body. In other words, the body mistakes its own tissue for a foreign substance and attacks itself. The most common treatment for autoimmune diseases today is to suppress the immune system with medications, especially with steroids such as cortisone.

L. E. Muñoz and colleagues from the University Hospital Erlangen in Germany supplied a new insight into vitamin D and autoimmune disorders when they found that most of the autoimmune disorders they studied involved vitamin D in one way or another.[22] What is the connection? What do 160 autoimmune diseases have in common with vitamin D?

According to C. E. Hayes and colleagues, a diverse and rapidly growing body of epidemiological, climatological, genetic, nutritional, and biological evidence indicates that the vitamin D system helps reduce the likelihood of the body attacking its own tissues and developing autoimmune disorders like autism.[23]

In 2012, G. A. Mostafa and colleagues reported that antibodies to brain tissue are common in autism and that those antibodies are inversely related to vitamin D levels: the higher the vitamin D level, the lower the antibody level.[24] They also reported that the rating scale for the severity of autism symptoms was directly related to vitamin D levels: the higher the vitamin D levels, the less severe the autism.

They also discovered something else, something overlooked in this discussion: the parents of the autistic children reported the same amount of sun exposure for their children as did the parents of the typically developing children. However, the vitamin D levels of the autistic children were much lower than those of the typically developing children. Such a study has never been repeated but implies that autistic children have a genetic defect (qualitative or quantitative) that gives them lower vitamin D levels. This is exactly what my theory would have predicted.

5. SEIZURE REDUCTION

Up to 25 percent of children with autism have seizures.[25] Correction of vitamin D deficiency helps control seizures, according to a recently published study.[26] A. Holló and colleagues measured baseline levels of vitamin D in 13 seizure patients.[26] Eight patients were extremely deficient, with average vitamin D levels less than 12 ng/mL. The investigators then corrected vitamin D deficiency in all 13 subjects, and 10 had a significant decrease in number of seizures.

6. TREG INCREASE

"Treg" sounds like a creature from *The Hobbit,* but actually, tregs, or T regulatory cells, are part of the immune system. Sometimes known as suppressor T cells, tregs calm the immune system, maintain tolerance to self, and reduce autoimmune disease. They help keep other immune cells from making errant antibodies. This self-stop is built into the immune system to prevent excessive untoward reactions, especially the ones that treat your own tissues like a foreign invader.

About four years ago, B. Prietl and Pieber wanted to see if vitamin D could increase the percentage of tregs;[27] if it could, it would mean that vitamin D might be effective in treating a whole range of autoimmune disorders. In a randomized controlled trial, they gave vitamin D to 46 healthy subjects and measured the tregs percentage at baseline and again at four and eight weeks. Sure enough, vitamin D significantly increased the percentage of tregs.

> Some experts feel that certain autoimmune disorders may be effectively treated with vitamin D.

Some experts feel that certain autoimmune disorders may be effectively treated with vitamin D via vitamin D's effect on immune cells, making the body less likely to attack itself.[28] Thus, vitamin D may help stop the autoimmune process in autism.

7. NEUROTROPHIN INCREASE

Neurotrophins are the family of proteins that help nerve and brain cells survive, develop, and function. Activated vitamin D increases neurotrophins up to fivefold.[29] Vitamin D deficiency in the uterus causes low levels of at least one important neurotrophin.[30] Thus, vitamin D appears to be intimately involved in regulating neurotrophins. Could it do the same in older autistic children, increasing neurotrophins and thus helping heal a damaged brain?

8. MITOCHONDRIAL PROTECTION

Mitochondria are the power plants of cells; every human cell has them. When they work properly, they transform sugar into an energy molecule called ATP. In autism, something is wrong with the mitochondria.[31] About 1 in 20 people with autism have obvious mitochondrial disease. Perhaps as many as 1 in 3 are in the gray zone: their mitochondria are not fully working. However, the numbers could be higher, as mild mitochondrial dysfunction is difficult to document.

Recently, I. M. Garcia and colleagues tested an activated vitamin D–like drug, paricalcitol, to see if it could protect mitochondria.[32] They purposefully injured mitochondria in two groups of lab animals—one group was given a placebo and the other was given activated vitamin D—by tying off the ureter (the tube connecting the kidney to the bladder). In the non–vitamin D group, the mitochondria interiors were larger and misshapen, indicating serious damage; these changes did not occur in the vitamin D group. In addition, markers of mitochondrial damage reverted to normal in paricalcitol-treated animals within several hours after the ureter was untied, but not in the control group.

These results suggest that vitamin D may have a protective effect at the mitochondrial level. Because vitamin D is turned into activated vitamin D in the tissues, it seems likely that vitamin D could protect mitochondria in people with autism.

9. DETOXIFICATION AND ANTIOXIDANT PRODUCTION

E. Garcion, from the Laboratory of Biochemistry and Molecular Biology in Angers, France, and others report that vitamin D increases production of glutathione, the master antioxidant and detoxification agent in the brain.[33–36] In fact, in a recent study of 693 adults at Emory University, blood levels of vitamin D and glutathione were directly associated, meaning the higher the vitamin D level, the higher the glutathione.[37] Because glutathione helps capture and excrete heavy metals (including mercury, a heavy metal at the heart of the vaccine controversy), vitamin D is involved in brain detoxification.[38]

H. D. Halicka and colleagues also found that several more proteins whose genes are increased by vitamin D are involved in detoxification.[4] Vitamin D upregulates a number of enzymes used to metabolize drugs, which the body treats as poison.[39]

Whether via DNA repair, anti-inflammatory actions, anti-autoimmune activities, anti-seizure activity, increase in regulatory T cells, mitochondrial protection, or stimulation of detoxification and antioxidant pathways, vitamin D stands ready to help your child. But is it safe to give your child vitamin D supplements? I tackle this topic in the next chapter.

Chapter Nine

High-Dose Vitamin D: Safe for My Child?

For parents, perhaps the most difficult aspect of giving their child vitamin D is the fear of poisoning, or toxicity—and it is a legitimate concern. It's one of the reasons I recommend regular blood tests in children on high doses of vitamin D. But the likelihood of overdosing on vitamin D is very low (with a couple of exceptions), provided you don't purposefully or accidentally take massive doses for long periods.

Government Recommendations and Upper Limits

If you've heard that vitamin D is toxic and can be fatal in overdose, you may be afraid to exceed the government recommendation—even if you are sick or dying from a disease associated with vitamin D deficiency. However, the current recommended level is woefully inadequate and is nothing more than a guideline to help people avoid bone-softening diseases such as osteomalacia and rickets. Scientists did not design these recommendations to prevent vitamin D deficiency but only to prevent these two bone diseases. When the government issued its recommendations in

2010,[1] it excluded all evidence except for that involving bone disease. It did not include any evidence about the role of vitamin D in diseases such as autism, influenza, heart disease, cancer, or asthma.

The 2010 meeting of the Institute of Medicine's Food and Nutrition Board set upper limits for children not being tested for vitamin D levels. By the board's own admission, these upper limits are lower than the scientific literature supports because the board was concerned about higher vitamin D intakes without the safety of regular blood tests. Thus, if you can't or won't get vitamin D blood tests for your child to guide dosage, do not exceed these daily upper-limit guidelines[2]:

- Ages 1 through 3: 2,500 units
- Ages 4 through 8: 3,000 units
- Ages 9 through 18: 4,000 units

The current upper limit for vitamin D no more impairs a physician's ability to treat vitamin D deficiency than comparable upper limits for calcium or magnesium impair her ability to treat those deficiencies. That is, the upper limits of the Food and Nutrition Board don't limit treatment of vitamin D deficiency when blood is being tested. They apply only to blind supplementation of vitamin D by people not under a doctor's care.

I always advise that calcidiol blood tests be used to guide dosing for any child taking high doses of vitamin D. I define "high dose" as any dose exceeding the Food and Nutrition Board's upper limit. Any child taking more than that requires periodic calcidiol blood tests. Knowing the calcidiol level educates the physician and the parents, not only about the safety of supplementation but also about the surprisingly high oral doses required to maintain high-normal levels.

DANGEROUS OR BENEFICIAL?

I understand why some people think that vitamin D is dangerous. That's exactly what I was taught in medical school. In fact, like most physicians my age, I left lectures in medical school believing that taking one extra multivitamin pill per day might cause vitamin D toxicity. That was the prevailing belief in the United States in the 1980s.

More recent studies and some older experiments show us otherwise. In fact, vitamin D is much safer than many common medications. Remember, vitamin D is not usually considered a medication; it's a naturally occurring nutrient that's freely available when you expose yourself to sunlight. However, you could consider it a medicine in that you should take vitamin D supplements in the correct dose, because extremely high amounts can be toxic or cause death.

British researchers gave community-dwelling older patients 100,000 units of vitamin D (the amount in 250 multivitamin pills) at once and repeated the dosage every four months for five years.[3] After taking a total of 15 million units of vitamin D, not a single patient showed any signs of toxicity. Instead, the vitamin D reduced their rate of fractures by about one-third, and the participants had a trend toward fewer deaths from illnesses such as cancer and heart disease. However, their calcidiol blood levels remained deficient, at only 29 ng/mL. Of course, 100,000 units over four months is an average of only about 800 units daily, which really is a small dose compared with the amount you need to maintain healthful levels. In addition, periodic large doses do not replicate the natural way humans made vitamin D for two million years, so doses must be daily to be natural.

That said, vitamin D can be fatal in overdose. Industrial manufacturing errors have caused most cases of vitamin D toxicity. In a few cases, thousands or even millions of times more vitamin D than was needed was added to milk or supplements. Unlike many prescription drugs, not one case of suicide by vitamin D has ever been reported. Accidental overdoses are exceedingly rare, and high doses of steroids used for treatment of toxicity may have caused some of the few reported deaths.

Aside from lab animal experiments and industrial accidents, much of what we know about vitamin D toxicity comes from reports of doctors who prescribed extreme doses of vitamin D for conditions such as hyperparathyroidism and osteoporosis. Even in these cases, few deaths occurred, although many patients had high blood calcium.

Although cases of toxicity are exceedingly rare in the medical literature, too much vitamin D, like too much water, can be lethal. But the chance of a physician seeing a patient who becomes ill from drinking too much water (water intoxication) is far more likely than a doctor ever seeing a patient with vitamin D toxicity. Ask your doctor if she has ever seen a case of water intoxication leading to death. Then ask if she's ever seen a case of vitamin D intoxication.

Almost 500 years ago, the father of toxicology (the science of poisoning), Paracelsus, wrote words that have rung true through the ages: "All things are poison, and nothing is without poison; only the dose permits something not to be poisonous."[4] For example, if you were to drink 80 glasses of water every day for a few days, you would end up in the emergency department and quickly learn that water is poisonous if taken in excessive doses. Vitamin D is not much different—it's just safer.

VITAMIN D TOXICITY VERSUS HYPERVITAMINOSIS D

Vitamin D blood levels above 100 ng/mL are abnormally high. Many people equate this with toxicity. It is not toxicity; it is hypervitaminosis D. That simply means the vitamin D level is elevated.

Having subclinical vitamin D toxicity means you have elevated vitamin D levels and high blood calcium. With this type of toxicity, there are no signs or symptoms; the patient feels fine.

Having clinical toxicity means you have elevated vitamin D levels (usually above 200 ng/mL), elevated blood calcium, and clinical symptoms such as loss of appetite, abdominal pain, nausea, weakness, frequent urination, and cardiac arrhythmias. Clinical toxicity is very rare.

Even many experts confuse hypervitaminosis D, subclinical toxicity, and clinical toxicity.

VITAMIN D TOXICITY IN CHILDREN

Vitamin D toxicity, especially subclinical toxicity, can occur, but it's easy to avoid if you know the results of your child's calcidiol blood test. Toxicity occurs as a result of high blood calcium, or hypercalcemia. When calcidiol levels exceed 150–200 ng/mL, the body's calcium levels slowly increase. Significant hypercalcemia occurs when calcium rises above 11 mg/dL (milligrams per deciliter).

Vitamin D toxicity usually occurs with hypercalcemia but without symptoms; it is preceded by high calcium levels in the urine, or hypercalcuria. In children, significant hypercalcemia generally requires vitamin D levels well in excess of 150 ng/mL for many months or years. Credible reports of vitamin D toxicity with significant hypercalcemia in older children consuming 20,000 units of vitamin D per day or fewer are absent in the medical literature. In fact, other than pharmaceutical manufacturing errors or dosing errors, the literature contains very few cases of vitamin D toxicity from supplement use; virtually all reported cases of hypercalcemia are from dosage errors, manufacturing errors, or patients treated medically with high doses of vitamin D_2.

The capacity of some children to process and use high doses of vitamin D is evident in a paper published in 2012. The author describes a 12-year-old girl who accidently received massive doses of vitamin D for months.[5] She was initially vitamin D–deficient, with a calcidiol level of 12 ng/mL. In error, she took 100,000 units of vitamin D daily for at least three months, for a total dose of at least 7.5 million units.

When the error was detected, her calcidiol level was 268 ng/mL, but her blood calcium level was normal (hypervitaminosis D). An ultrasound of her kidneys showed no evidence of calcium deposits. She had no symptoms of clinical toxicity. The vitamin D was stopped, and she felt fine throughout the episode.

This is not to say that the dose was safe; it was not. Eventually, the toxic dose may have sickened her. This just illustrates that, in the short run, some children appear to have a significant ability to process huge doses of vitamin D.

Another example of the relative safety—and paradoxes—of high daily doses of vitamin D in children comes from Finland. From 1952 to 1964, the Finnish government recommended 4,000 units daily for all infants. In 1964, the government reduced the recommendation to 2,000 units per day; in 1975, to 1,000 units and, in 1992, to 400 units.[6]

Although 4,000 units per day in infancy may cause mild hyper-calcemia, I am unaware of any reports in the Finnish literature indicating that it did. The literature does show that Finnish infants who took high-dose vitamin D were nine times less likely than those who didn't to develop type 1 diabetes.[6] Baby boys so supplemented were 12 times less likely than those who didn't receive supplements to have schizophrenia later in life.[7] Based on the lack of reports in the medical literature, autism was apparently exceedingly rare in Finland during the years of high-dose supplementation of infants and children.

Another way to see the relative safety of vitamin D is to look at a country that used a high single dose to prevent vitamin D deficiency in infants.[8] In France, physician scientists gave infants 15, 5, or 2.5 mg as a single dose. Remember, 40,000 units equals 1 mg, so the infants got 600,000, 200,000, or 100,000 units as a single dose.

The infants who received 600,000 units had calcidiol levels of 122 ng/mL two weeks after the dose. Vitamin D levels above 100 ng/mL were found in half of the infants given 600,000 units, but prolonged hypercalcemia was not found, only transient mild hypercalcemia in a few of the infants given the largest dose. Certainly, 600,000 units is too much for an infant, yet the dosage caused no significant toxicity.

In 1982 in Germany, doctors gave 16 newborns 1,000 units per day to prevent rickets. After six weeks of treatment, calcidiol values were 54 ng/mL,[9] right in the middle of the normal range. If you multiply that by five and assume such infants weighed 10 pounds at birth, a 50-pound child taking 5,000 units per day should expect a calcidiol level of about 54 ng/mL after six weeks, depending on the baseline level, which is in line with what parents report.

From 1959 to 1991, pediatricians gave all infants and toddlers in East Germany 600,000 units of vitamin D every three months until they reached 18 months.[10] A few cases of high blood calcium occurred after the dosing, but no clinical complications were reported.

VITAMIN D TOXICITY AND PREGNANCY

Unwarranted fear of toxicity is the main reason that vitamin D deficiency in pregnancy is an ongoing problem.[11] Pregnant women or women thinking of becoming pregnant should have their calcidiol levels checked. Obstetricians should advise pregnant women to supplement appropriately based on their blood levels.

Recently, the Canadian Paediatric Society recommended that all pregnant women take at least 2,000 units per day—an improvement but certainly still inadequate.[12] Bruce Hollis and Carol Wagner, experts in the vitamin D requirements of pregnant or lactating women, recommended that pregnant women take, at the very least, 4,000 units daily.[13] They predict that such doses will help prevent numerous undesired birth outcomes, such as infection, prematurity, toxemia of pregnancy, and cesarean birth.

Pregnant women who take only a prenatal vitamin, with its 400–600 units of vitamin D, are placing both themselves and their fetuses at risk. My recommendation is that pregnant women take 6,000 units per day—5,000 units for the woman (as for all adults) and 1,000 units for her fetus. Pregnant women who obtain calcidiol levels on that dose will discover that their levels are in the mid range.

SOMETIMES VITAMIN D IS NOT RECOMMENDED

In a few situations, sunlight or vitamin D supplementation may make a condition worse; in these cases, it is not recommended.

Toxicity or Allergy

The only absolute contraindication to vitamin D supplementation is vitamin D toxicity or allergy to vitamin D, although—to the best of my knowledge—there are no reports in the literature of acute allergic reactions to vitamin D supplements. However, some people are allergic to the gelatin in the capsules. In this case, they should empty the contents of the capsule into a glass of water and drink it.

MY HUSBAND IS INTERACTING WITH OUR SON AGAIN

Dear Dr. Cannell:

I learned about the vitamin D link with autism and started supplementing my 12-year-old son because it is such a cheap, easy, and low-risk thing to do. I wanted so much to be able to help him, yet I was afraid to have hope.

My son has Asperger's-type autism and oppositional defiant disorder. He's always been an indoor kid. He is a redhead and burns easily, and I've always protected him from the sun. I started him on 5,000 IU of vitamin D (he is starting puberty and weighs almost 110 pounds). He has much social dysfunction, self-stimulatory behavior (e.g., belly smacking, hair pulling, nail biting), paranoia, attention problems, difficulty with group dynamics and, of course, an obsession with computers. My husband was so discouraged by our son's negativity that he stopped interacting with him.

My son's doctors implied that there is no hope and think vitamin D is nonsense. But we started giving him 5,000 IU of vitamin D daily. After two months, his behavior improved in almost all areas. He started doing much better in school behavior-wise and earned his privileges back in several areas. My husband is even starting to interact with him again.

Sincerely,

Terry

Dear Terry:

There is always hope. However, your doctor needs to measure his vitamin D levels. The 5,000 IU/day that you are giving him is probably not enough to obtain high-normal levels in a 110-pound adolescent. Seventy-five percent of parents report improvement with vitamin D levels at about 80 ng/mL.

As far as "'daring to hope,"' I am so glad, because too many doctors rely on only conclusive studies to treat patients. Oliver Wendell Holmes, the nineteenth-century physician and poet, once said, "Physicians have many rights, but the right to take away hope is not among them."

John Cannell, MD

Skin Conditions

Reasons to avoid sunlight or artificial ultraviolet radiation include a number of dermatological conditions. The parent of a child with rashes should ask his physician if sunlight should be avoided with the particular rash. Skin conditions that might be an issue include polymorphous light eruption, lupus, porphyria, photosensitivity dermatitis, and albinism.

INCREASED SENSITIVITY TO VITAMIN D

Vitamin D hypersensitivity syndromes are not vitamin D toxicity. Rather, they occur when kidney tissues overproduce calcitriol, causing hypercalcemia. These syndromes are diagnosed by measuring calcium (elevated), calcidiol (normal or low), and calcitriol (elevated). Vitamin D hypersensitivity syndromes can occur in primary hyperparathyroidism, diseases such as sarcoidosis and tuberculosis, and some lymphomas.

Vitamin D hypersensitivity syndromes are more much common than vitamin D toxicity; treatment of vitamin D deficiency in people with hypercalcemia should be approached with caution. They are exceedingly rare in children. People with hypercalcemia should avoid vitamin D until the cause of the high blood calcium is clarified. Once the cause is clear, if physicians decide to treat the accompanying vitamin D deficiency—despite the hypercalcemia— they should do so only if the hypercalcemia is mild to moderate (less than 12 mg/dL). They should also proceed cautiously, frequently monitoring calcium, calcidiol, and calcitriol.

How Much Have You Learned?

The following questions will help you digest the information in this chapter. How many can you answer correctly?

1. One of the world's foremost authorities on vitamin D metabolism and physiology said, "Worrying about vitamin D toxicity is like worrying about drowning when you are dying of thirst." True or false?

   True. In 1999, Reinhold Vieth wrote a review of the literature, debunking fears of vitamin D toxicity.[14] This was the paper that started me on my vitamin D journey, a "must read" for anyone interested in vitamin D. It is available for free on the Internet (http://ajcn.nutrition.org/content/69/5/842.full); I have read the paper at least 10 times and get something new out of it each time.

2. How much vitamin D would it take to permanently harm a child?

   No one knows. However, in 2005, doctors at the University of Maryland School of Medicine found out how much it takes to sicken a child. They reported a case of a child who accidentally overdosed on vitamin D.[15]

   The mother had given her 32-pound son liquid Raquiferol, a vitamin D supplement made in Latin America. The directions stated that adults should take 2,500–5,000 units per day, but the child took at least 600,000 units daily for four days (2,400,000 units, or 60 mg). He had stomach pain, mild high blood pressure, and high blood calcium but made an uneventful recovery once the doctors identified the cause. So we still don't know how much it takes to permanently injure a child.

Doctors say that 21 mg/kg (milligrams per kilogram) of body weight per day is the average lethal dose in rats. If the same is true in humans, a 25 kg (55-pound) child would require more than five million units—about a thousand 5,000-unit pills daily. It would be difficult to get anyone, let alone a child, to consume that many pills in a day. Regardless, the child in question became quite ill by taking one-fifth of that amount (4 mg/kg). His blood calcium peaked at 15 mg/dL—high enough to cause death. To get that sick, a child weighing 55 pounds would probably have to take 12 mg per day for several days: about 500,000 units, or a hundred 5,000-unit capsules.

3. Water has a safer therapeutic index (the average lethal dose divided by the average effective dose) than vitamin D. True, false, or they are about the same?
   False. Precise human studies of the lethality of vitamin D have never been done (for obvious ethical reasons). However, water intoxication, which leads to very low blood sodium, brain swelling and, on occasion, death, is not uncommon.[16] Water intoxication could occur if you drank 80 glasses of water daily for several days rather than the usual eight glasses. That is, the therapeutic index of water is about 10 (80 divided by 8).

   Robert Heaney demonstrated that healthy humans use about 5,000 units of vitamin D daily if they get it.[17] Ten times that amount, 50,000 units per day, for several months is certainly not acutely toxic, so the therapeutic index of vitamin D is greater than 10. In fact, a study in *The New England Journal of Medicine* indicated that young, fair-skinned people receive more than 50,000 units from one sunburn.[18]

4. If a five-year-old, 40-pound child totally avoided the sun and regularly took a standard multivitamin containing 400 units of vitamin D daily for several years as his sole source of vitamin D, he would:

    a. Rapidly become vitamin D–toxic and require medical attention for symptoms of hypercalcemia

    b. Slowly become vitamin D–toxic and eventually have symptoms

    c. Slowly develop hypercalcemia but have no symptoms

    d. Obtain a healthful vitamin D blood level

    e. Become vitamin D–deficient

The answer is e. A standard multivitamin contains 400 units of vitamin D, which is inadequate for a five-year-old child. If one totally avoids the sun, as many dermatologists now recommend, 400 units daily would be enough vitamin D to prevent vitamin D–deficient rickets, but the child would still have low vitamin D blood levels and be at risk for numerous other chronic diseases.[19]

    The key to the above statement is the clause "if one totally avoids the sun." Most people who do not purposefully expose themselves to the sun still get much of their vitamin D from casual sun exposure, such as sunlight that strikes their faces, arms, and hands in the few minutes it takes to walk to the car or get the mail.[20] Of course, some people follow their doctor's advice and take obsessive steps to prevent sunlight from striking their unprotected skin. A host of diseases awaits those who follow such advice, especially if they don't take meaningful quantities of vitamin D in the form of supplements.[21]

5. Of the medications below, which is the safest in overdose if 250 tablets or capsules are taken at once?

a. Vitamin D, 1,000-unit capsules

b. Aspirin, 325-mg tablets

c. Acetaminophen (Tylenol), 500-mg tablets

The answer is a. In fact, a comparable dose of hundreds of thousands of units of vitamin D at one time is called stoss therapy, which is used, especially in Europe, to treat vitamin D deficiency. (For a review of many studies and the doses needed to achieve toxic 25-OH vitamin D levels, see Vieth's 1999 article.[14])

6. Which of the following is safest in overdose?

    a. Lithium

    b. Coumadin

    c. Dilantin

    d. Vitamin D

The answer is d. All the other medications can be deadly in overdose.[22] That's not true for vitamin D, mainly because a huge number of capsules would be needed for an overdose (excluding the 50,000-unit capsule).

7. By sunbathing for a few minutes in the noonday summer sun, you can, without any unwanted side effects, easily obtain five times the vitamin D toxicity upper limit recommended by the Institute of Medicine's Food and Nutrition Board. True or false? *True, at least for fair-skinned people.* The Food and Nutrition Board lists the daily upper limit as 4,000 units for vitamin D for adults, but the "no observed adverse effects level" (the amount that scientific studies confirm is safe for adults) is 10,000 units. Studies show that young, fair-skinned people usually make as many as 20,000 units in a single, full-body

sunlight session that leads to pink skin.[18] Numerous factors affect the body's ability to make such high amounts of vitamin D, mainly genetics, weight, age, skin type, latitude, clothing, season, and sunscreen use.

8. In a case of vitamin D toxicity described in *The New England Journal of Medicine,* a man recovered uneventfully after taking a health supplement that contained 156,000 units of vitamin D_3 daily for two years. True or false?
   True.[23] Actually, he probably took more than that. An industrial manufacturing error was implicated. Such reports help confirm what is known from laboratory animal data; that is, it takes a lot of vitamin D to hurt you.

9. Acute poisoning leading to rapid death from ingestion of vitamin D capsules:
   a. Has often been reported in the literature
   b. Has occasionally been reported in the literature
   c. Has never been reported in the literature
   The answer is c, as far as I know. I do know of one interesting case that demonstrates the relative safety of vitamin D. Industrial-strength crystalline vitamin D was added to table sugar, either by accident or on purpose, and two men who consumed the sugar took in about 1,700,000 units of vitamin D_3 daily for seven months—425 times the federal government's current daily upper limit.[24] Both became quite ill but fully recovered after the cause was identified. With autistic children who have their vitamin D blood levels checked regularly, such an event could not occur. First, no child would get such a dose. Second, no autistic child taking adult doses would go seven months without a blood test.

10. If a healthy adult tried to kill himself by taking an entire bottle (100 capsules) of 5,000 units of vitamin D (a total of 500,000 units), which of the following would happen?

    a. He would die within 24 hours from severely elevated blood calcium levels and widespread calcium deposits

    b. He might survive with intensive treatment for high blood calcium

    c. High blood calcium would be severe but would require only supportive treatment

    d. The dose would be a minor health benefit

The answer is d. A dose of 500,000 units (about 12 mg) may give a one-time boost to vitamin D levels, but the body would use it in several months. Blood levels would not stay adequate for long.

Chapter Ten

My Recommendations for Vitamin D, Sunlight, Other Supplements and Diet

In my opinion, treating some symptoms of autism might be as simple as aggressively raising calcidiol blood levels to high-normal. Although, at the time of this writing, I do not have controlled studies to prove that vitamin D effectively treats autism symptoms, I've referenced many studies that support the theory.

I've included testimonials from parents who've seen remarkable improvements in their children with high doses of vitamin D. I've also explained, in commonsense terms, the correlation between the first large wave of ASD cases and the emergence of sun avoidance (i.e., vitamin D deficiency). I have described how vitamin D works. Finally, I've explained that raising vitamin D levels to high-normal can't hurt and may provide health benefits beyond improving autistic symptoms.

I believe that raising calcidiol blood levels to high-normal is safe and without significant risk. Not doing so means you will never know whether this simple and inexpensive solution might help. So a risk-benefit analysis favors high vitamin D levels. You make a risk-benefit analysis every time you put your child in your car, knowing he could be injured in an accident. Using adult doses of vitamin D with frequent blood tests carries little risk, so such an analysis favors using vitamin D.

Treating with vitamin D is simple. It's relatively inexpensive and requires little time on your part. The right vitamin D_3 supplement is available over the counter or online—don't use a vitamin D_2 prescription (Drisdol) from your doctor. With a little help from 25(OH)D blood tests—preferably administered at your doctor's office or an in-home blood test kit available through the Vitamin D Council—and from the guidelines offered in this chapter, you and your healthcare provider can effectively administer supplements and monitor your child's vitamin D levels.

The first step is to bring this book to your doctor and ask that your child's calcidiol blood level be tested or go to vitamindcouncil.org and order in-home blood tests. If your child's vitamin D is below the high-normal range, your child may benefit from vitamin D supplementation. In autistic children, the goal is to raise calcidiol levels to high-normal.

Most American labs list normal calcidiol levels as 30–100 ng/mL, so high-normal is 80 ng/mL. Some labs use different testing methods and list the normal range as 20–75 ng/mL. In such cases, try to obtain levels around 65 ng/mL. In all cases, the goal is simply to be high-normal.

No physician should tell you that a high-normal vitamin D level is harmful. If a physician tells you the dose is toxic, insist on having a 25(OH)D and calcium blood test drawn immediately. In toxicity, calcidiol is above 200 ng/mL and blood calcium is elevated. Virtually all autistic people test low for vitamin D and need to take vitamin D_3 supplements, as most of them are not in the sun long enough to raise vitamin D levels to high-normal ranges.

Following the suggestions in this book requires frequent blood tests for vitamin D levels in your child, as the dose required for a possible effect is much higher than that usually recommended for children. Ideally, the entire program should be under the supervision of a healthcare provider. Because virtually the entire program to obtain high-normal vitamin D levels in autistic children can be done by parents, parents may be tempted to achieve such levels on their own. I discourage this, because high-normal vitamin D levels are close to abnormally high levels, although a significant safety margin exists between abnormally high (hypervitaminosis D) and toxic levels.

Frequent blood level testing is indispensable when treating vitamin D deficiency with high doses of vitamin D, because neither age nor weight can accurately predict dose response or how high levels will go

> Frequent blood level testing is indispensable when treating vitamin D deficiency with high doses of vitamin D.

with any particular dose, as responses vary widely among children. This is why high doses should never be given unless vitamin D levels are being closely monitored.

Keep in mind that these vitamin D doses exceed the upper limit set by the Food and Nutrition Board and the US government. Do not proceed unless you fully understand that. In fact, the doses are closer to high adult doses (3,000–15,000 IU/day), sometimes even higher, just to obtain high-normal levels in autistic children.

Also keep in mind that high-normal levels are still normal levels and that the vitamin D levels recommended in this book have been obtained by sun exposure alone. The information that follows is for you and your child's healthcare provider.

DOSAGE AND SUPPLEMENTATION

As with most supplements and medicines, initial dosages are determined by body weight. Because it is extremely difficult to overdose on vitamin D, let's start with a standard initial dosage. Monitor 25(OH)D blood tests every three months and adjust the dose accordingly. In most cases, to effectively obtain high-normal blood levels of vitamin D in vitamin D–deficient children, you need to use adult doses (5,000–15,000 IU/day). Obese and older children might need an even higher dose.

Parents are understandably concerned about using such doses in children. However, with vitamin D, blood level determines dose, so if your child's vitamin D levels are high-normal, your dosage is correct. As a safety measure, the higher the dose, the more frequently you should check calcidiol levels. When in doubt, always measure the calcidiol level to be sure the dose is right.

You or your child's healthcare provider should measure calcidiol levels every three months until she figures out how much your child needs to maintain about 80 ng/mL year round. (Again, you can get in-home vitamin D blood tests online at www.vitamindcouncil.org.)

Over the course of a couple of years, you'll have a good idea of any seasonal changes you need to make to maintain your child's level in the high-normal range. The dose that seems to help is the dose that raises the autistic individual's vitamin D levels to high-normal. If it takes 2,000 IU/day to do that, 2,000 IU/day is the correct dose. If it takes 15,000 IU/day to do that, 15,000 IU/day is the correct dose. It comes down to trial and error, using vitamin D blood tests to be sure you're not giving your child too much or too little.

It is not just weight and age that determine dosage. Genetics plays a big part, so no one can accurately predict how much vitamin D your child needs to obtain high-normal levels. With older or obese children or adults, doses of 10,000–15,000 IU/day are sometimes necessary. Again, you and your doctor will know the dose is safe (and adequate) if the blood level stays within the high-normal range.

MARGIN FOR ERROR

Any fears you might have about high doses are understandable. But when supplementing with vitamin D, you've got a wide berth for error. What happens if the blood level exceeds 100 ng/mL, for instance? Usually, nothing at all.

High blood calcium is possible with calcidiol levels above 150–200 ng/mL. This is perfectly safe in the short term, provided the hypercalcemia is mild and the dosage of vitamin D is promptly decreased.

Mildly elevated blood calcium is dangerous only if it goes undetected. Even then, the chance of it permanently damaging internal organs such as the kidneys is very small.

Testing your child's calcidiol levels every three months will alert you if blood levels become too high. If levels are above 100 ng/mL, simply lower the dosage.

VITAMIN D SUPPLEMENTS

Vitamin D supplements are a must for autistic children. The only vitamin D supplement you should consider taking is vitamin D_3 (cholecalciferol). I recommend D_3Plus (which I formulated), available online at www.vitamindcouncil.org. However, any vitamin D_3 supplement will do. Proper doses of vitamin D_3 supplements are now widely available in pharmacies. Do not take the prescription vitamin D_2 (Drisdol); it is not the same as vitamin D_3.

Large amounts of vitamin D_3 are produced naturally in the skin on exposure to sunlight. To duplicate vitamin D production in the skin by the sun, you need much larger quantities of oral vitamin D than the federal government recommends. But 25(OH)D blood tests will teach you that. The vitamin D_3 in supplements is purified from radiated, ground-up animal skins that are then meticulously processed, purified, measured, and put into liquid, capsules, or tablets. Vegetarians and vegans should either get their vitamin D from the sun or use Vitashine (available on the Internet).

You can buy 50,000-IU capsules of vitamin D_3 without a prescription online. These capsules are potentially dangerous; they are about two times more potent than 50,000-IU capsules of D_2. Vitamin D_3 in this quantity should be considered a medicine, not a supplement. Do not give either type of 50,000-IU capsule to your child.

The only vitamin D supplement you should consider taking is vitamin D_3.

Also, some doctors mistakenly prescribe other vitamin D–like drugs. Activated vitamin D (calcitriol; sometimes sold under the brand name Rocaltrol) and similar preparations (Hectorol and Zemplar) are the most commonly misused vitamin D drugs. They are different from vitamin D_3 in that they are not building blocks but active steroids. These drugs have certain approved medical indications, mainly for the treatment of renal failure. They do not treat vitamin D deficiency or autism, and a physician who prescribes them for vitamin D deficiency is incompetent. The only compound that should be used for treating vitamin D–deficient autistic children is vitamin D_3.

Initial Dosage

The amount of vitamin D needed initially varies with body weight, body fat, age, skin color, season, latitude, baseline calcidiol levels, and sunning habits. Thus, the recommendations below are only ballpark estimates; your child may need more. Everyone is different. The bullet list below is meant to help you and your healthcare provider. Copy it and take it (or the entire book) with you to the doctor's office.

Remember, any vitamin D supplement will do if it is the proper dosage and the child has proper nutritional intake of vitamin D's essential cofactors (see "Vitamin D Cofactors" on page 136). If the child cannot swallow capsules, cut open the D$_3$Plus capsules with scissors and dissolve the contents in a smoothie. Otherwise, I recommend using Ddrops, available widely on the Internet.

> The amount of vitamin D needed initially varies with body weight, body fat, age, skin color, season, latitude, baseline calcidiol levels, and sunning habits.

As a general rule, autistic children who will be getting regular vitamin D blood tests need to start with the dose listed below. However, estimates based on weight must take into account children who are very efficient makers of calcidiol, so these estimates are too low for some children to see a significant treatment effect. Nonetheless, my starting recommendations are:

- Children weighing less than 33 pounds
    1,600 IU/day (one capsule D$_3$Plus)
- Children weighing 33–66 pounds
    3,300 IU/day (two capsules D$_3$Plus)
- Children weighing 66–100 pounds
    5,000 IU/day (three capsules D$_3$Plus)

After three months, adjust the dose accordingly. If the blood level is above 80 ng/mL, lower the dose. If it is below 80 ng/mL, increase the dose.

Usually, it takes 5,000–15,000 IU/day to obtain high-normal vitamin D levels in most autistic children.

THE IMPORTANCE OF BLOOD TESTS

You will never know your child's vitamin D level unless you have it tested. Your healthcare provider is your best source, but you can buy test kits online at vitamindcouncil. org. A few days after you order it, the test kit, including instructions, will arrive by mail. Be sure to watch the online video before attempting to obtain blood from your child. After watching the video, use the lancet to collect several drops of your child's blood. The more spots on the blotter paper you fill, the better, but two or three drops are enough. Fill out the paperwork and send everything back in the envelope provided. In about 10–14 days, you will know your child's vitamin D level.

If a 25(OH)D test result seems out of line (higher than you expect), repeat it right away. For instance, if your child weighs 75 pounds and is taking only 1,600 IU/day but her level is 110 ng/mL (high), repeat the blood test. The level is almost certainly a lab error. If the second test comes back high, reduce the vitamin D and have the level checked again right away using a different laboratory.

If your child responds and the response is long lived, find the lowest effective dose by slowly reducing the vitamin D. That is, a child who responds to 5,000 IU/day may do just as well on 3,300 IU/day. You always want to use the lowest effective dose. If the child

> You will never know your child's vitamin D level unless you have it tested.

worsens on the lower dose, resume the higher dose, remembering that frequent 25(OH)D tests are a must.

Elevated Blood Vitamin D Level

If the test shows an elevated blood level of vitamin D, do not panic. Toxicity usually begins to occur only when calcidiol levels exceed 200 ng/mL, so an upper limit of 100 ng/mL gives you a lot of leeway.

It is important to remember that you cannot accurately estimate calcidiol levels from the dose due to genetically determined differences in the metabolism of vitamin D. Therefore, your child's blood level may go above 100 ng/mL, the upper limit in most labs. Levels above 100 ng/mL not associated with high blood calcium are simply hypervitaminosis D.

This is not a disaster. If you were to measure your child's blood calcium level, it would probably be normal (less than 11mg/dL). This elevation in calcidiol is not dangerous in the short run. If it were to go on for years, it might elevate blood calcium (hypercalcemia) or urine calcium (hypercalciuria).

But, as a recent review stated, "There is little evidence from existing trials that vitamin D above current reference intakes is harmful. In most trials, reports of hypercalcemia and hypercalciuria were not associated with clinically relevant events."[1] No one has ever described such damage, nor has anyone ever described significantly elevated blood calcium levels in children with calcidiol levels above 100 ng/mL but below 150 ng/mL.

Rarely, mild elevations of blood calcium have been described with lower calcidiol levels, but these mildly elevated blood calcium levels used to be classified as normal, so their significance is questionable.[1] At any rate, any time vitamin D levels are above 100 ng/mL, take steps to reduce the vitamin D, even if your child's autism symptoms are responding well with the higher calcidiol levels.

Resistance from Your Physician

Many doctors will be alarmed at the amount of vitamin D you want your child to take and will recommend no more than 400 IU/day. If a doctor tells you that the dose you want is dangerous, ask for an immediate vitamin D blood test and point out that the level you're aiming for is in the high-normal range.

If you don't want this hassle, go to the Vitamin D Council's website (www.vitamindcouncil.org) and order a kit to check your child's blood at home. (Note that Maryland and New York do not allow in-home testing.)

Sunlight Exposure

I recommend what humans have done for two million years—expose lots of the skin to ultraviolet light without sunscreen. I believe science does not know everything and that nature is seldom wrong. The job of science is to reveal the mysteries of nature. If you avoid ultraviolet light completely, you are taking an unnecessary risk.

If you do choose to have your child sunbathe, remember, for most light-skinned adults, 20 minutes of full-body, summer, mid-day sun exposure puts more than 10,000 IU of vitamin D into circulation, so most children get about 5,000 IU in the same conditions.

Be careful in the spring when you first take your child outside. Be sure she does not burn. Try sunbathing for short periods in mid-day beginning in early April and ending in the middle of September (according to your geographical location).

When you start in the spring, have your child spend only 2–15 minutes on each side, front and back, depending on her skin type.

Go outside around solar noon (when the sun is at its highest point) and have her wear only a bathing suit—less if possible. Soon your child will develop the healthy tan that the US government used to recommend for all children.

> Be careful in the spring when you first take your child outside. Be sure she does not burn.

For autistic children, sunlight alone is most likely not enough. A child who lives in the northern United States cannot obtain vitamin D via sunlight during the "vitamin D winter." Even those who live in southern states may find it difficult to get enough sunlight in winter, as the sun is often too low on the horizon. Many dark-skinned children do not get the extra time they need to get vitamin D from sunlight. Vitamin D supplements are crucial for people with autism, and exposure to sunlight remains an important part of the treatment program.

Seasonal Supplementation

Oral supplements appear to work more quickly in the late spring and summer than in the fall or winter due to increasing incidental skin production of vitamin D during the warmer months. For example, supplementation with 1,600 IU/day in the autumn may appear to have little effect on calcidiol levels that are already in the 30s.

Such levels may even decline slightly in the fall and winter months—despite supplementation with 2,000 IU/day—due to the body's continued use of stored vitamin D combined with reduced skin vitamin D production during the colder months. Likewise, supplementation in the spring may result in higher-than-expected calcidiol levels due to the cumulative effects of supplementation and increased sun exposure in the warmer months.

Vitamin D and Sunburn

Is your child's skin sensitive to the sun? In the spring, does she get sunburned after minimal sun exposure? Anecdotal evidence suggests that a pleasant surprise may await you when her calcidiol levels go above 50 ng/mL: her skin may become less sensitive to the sun, and she may tan more easily. (But she can still sunburn.) I have received dozens of emails from readers of my newsletter confirming this observation.

My daughter, Eliza, noticed this change as a teenager. She had been taking 5,000 IU/day for about a year when she decided to begin tanning. She noticed two things. First, she did not burn early in the year as she usually did. Second, she quickly developed a dark, rich tan.

After she told me this, I asked a close friend who goes river rafting every spring to try an experiment. He is blond and blue-eyed and, despite applying sunscreen frequently, the bright spring sunlight reflecting off the water burns his face. I sent him 14 50,000-IU capsules of vitamin D_3 and asked him to take one capsule per day for two weeks before he went rafting. He wasn't convinced. He still used sunscreen.

At the end of a day on the river, his face was red, but the next morning the redness was gone—no sunburn. After a week on the river, he bore the type of tan he usually developed only at the end of the summer.

SUNLIGHT VERSUS SUPPLEMENTATION

To obtain ideal benefits, I recommend both vitamin D supplements and direct exposure to the sun via safe, sensible sun sessions, taking care not to burn. Exposing the body to sunlight is natural and simply replicates one of the conditions when humans first became humans, before autism became epidemic.

If you live above 30 degrees latitude, sunbathe your child and use supplements in the spring and summer; in the fall and winter, use vitamin D supplements only but increase the dose. If you live below 30 degrees latitude, sunbathe and use supplements year around.

As far as sunbathing goes, we know that sunlight tends to damage the skin if we stay out too long, just as water damages us if we drink too much of it. However, I believe that the skin needs ultraviolet light just as the body needs water.

> Exposing the body to sunlight is natural and simply replicates one of the conditions when humans first became humans, before autism became epidemic.

♦

WHAT'S YOUR CHILD'S SKIN TYPE?

From spring to fall (depending on where you live), the length of time your child should stay in the sun depends on his skin type. Dermatologists classify skin types with number designations from I to VI.

Those with type I skin are very fair, with green or blue eyes and, often, red hair. People with type I skin almost never tan and often have freckles from previous sun exposure. People from Greece and the Middle East with olive skin have skin type III. Type VI skin is shiny black, with high reflectance. People with this skin type trace their ancestry to tropical regions of Africa or India. A skin type VI almost never burns.

No matter what skin type you have, you'll never burn if you stay in the sun for about half the time it takes for your skin to begin to turn pink. Most people have a good idea of how long that is, but if you don't know, stay out for only a few minutes of exposure and increase the period until you do know. For a type I, that might be only several minutes. For a type VI, it might be several hours.

Skin type	Reaction to the sun
I	Always burns, never tans, sensitive ("Celtic")
II	Burns easily, tans minimally ("Northern European")
III	Burns moderately, tans gradually to light brown (average white)
IV	Burns minimally, always tans to moderate brown (olive skin)
V	Rarely burns, tans to dark (brown skin)
VI	Never burns, deeply pigmented, not sensitive (black skin)

WARNING:
EXTRA VITAMIN A MAY IMPAIR VITAMIN D ACTIONS

To work properly, vitamin D requires a vitamin A molecule, but if your child's system carries too much vitamin A, it interferes with vitamin D's ability to improve brain performance.

Recent studies indicate that subclinical (without signs or symptoms) vitamin A toxicity is a problem in developed countries, especially the United States.[2] The main offender is preformed retinol, such as retinyl acetate or retinyl palmitate, taken as a supplement, in multivitamins, cod liver oil, or fortified foods.

Other culprits include an acne medication formerly called Accutane. And 16 nutrition experts recently warned about the dangers of vitamin A toxicity and cod liver oil.[3]

VITAMIN D COFACTORS

Vitamin D needs dozens of cofactors—substances essential for the activity of an enzyme—to work properly. Cofactors are needed for metabolizing vitamin D. Deficiency in these cofactors is relatively rare, except for four of them: magnesium, zinc, boron, and vitamin K_2. One reason I like D_3Plus is that it contains all of these cofactors.

Magnesium

In a healthy body, magnesium is the fourth most abundant mineral. It is required in each of the steps of replication, transcription, and translation of genetic information. Thus, it is also needed for the genetic vitamin D system to function. All enzymes that metabolize vitamin D, turning it into a steroid hormone, need magnesium to work properly.[4] In fact, more than 300 enzymes in the body require magnesium.[5] Studies show that many Americans have deficient intakes of magnesium.[6] Unfortunately, most doctors continue to think a magnesium blood test can be used to detect deficiency. However, such tests do not detect mild to moderate whole-body magnesium deficiencies, because blood magnesium is carefully regulated by the body, as is blood calcium.

Magnesium is at the heart of the chlorophyll molecule, the pigment that makes plants green; green leafy vegetables are rich in magnesium. Other good sources are nuts, seeds, whole grains, dried fruit, and some fish. The richest source by far on a per-gram basis is dried seeds (e.g., pumpkin, sunflower, sesame), which contain about 200 mg per 100-g serving. High-magnesium foods were probably dietary staples of our Paleolithic ancestors.

Apparently, magnesium is better absorbed from foods than from supplements, and absorption varies with the degree of deficiency. What is not known is how mild to moderate total body magnesium deficiencies (which most Americans apparently have) affect vitamin D metabolism.

The safe thing to do is to eat green, leafy vegetables and a handful of sunflower seeds every day. This helps supply the body with the magnesium that vitamin D needs, but it is not enough to treat magnesium deficiency; for this, your child should take a magnesium supplement containing a minimum of 125–500 mg magnesium, depending on weight, for at least six months.

Zinc

The human body requires zinc. Zinc deficiency affects about two billion people worldwide and is associated with many diseases. Zinc is found primarily in plants, but the concentration varies with levels of the element in the soil. When adequate zinc is in the soil, food plants such as wheat (germ and bran) and various seeds contain the most zinc. Zinc is also found in beans and nuts.

Zinc deficiency is usually due to insufficient dietary intake but can be associated with malabsorption, autism, and other chronic illnesses, including mental illnesses.[7,8] No studies have assessed the effect of vitamin D on zinc deficiencies, but zinc is an important vitamin D cofactor.

> Zinc deficiency affects about two billion people worldwide and is associated with many diseases.

Studies show that zinc deficiencies are particularly common in autism.[9] In one study, investigators examined zinc concentrations in hair in nearly 2,000 children with ASD. One-fourth of the children had very low zinc levels, while the incidence of zinc deficiency in these children was slightly more than 50 percent.[9] The authors reported that zinc deficiency may contribute to autism and that zinc supplementation may help.

I recommend at least 12 mg supplemental zinc daily for all autistic children, because this amount corrects the deficiency and does no harm. This is a safe dose for all children and so does not require a blood test.

Boron

Little research has been done on boron, but because it is contained in plants, seeds, and nuts, boron deficiency is probably not uncommon. Boron is involved in vitamin D's rapid action on the cell wall.[10] Like magnesium, boron is present in vegetables or foods produced from plants.

Some scientists think boron plays several biochemical roles in humans via vitamin D.[11] Although boron is not considered an essential element, its presence in the body and influences on many metabolic enzymes make some scientists think it's essential. It is involved in the metabolism of steroid hormones such as activated vitamin D, as well as in the metabolism of magnesium and calcium.[12] When postmenopausal women took 3 mg of boron per day, their excretion of calcium was reduced by 44 percent, suggesting a direct or indirect interaction with vitamin D.[13]

> Some scientists think boron plays several biochemical roles in humans via vitamin D.

I recommend that autistic children take 2 mg of supplemental boron per day, which can do no harm and supplies adequate boron.

Vitamin K_2

The vitamin found in green, leafy vegetables (K_1) is well-known, especially in relationship to blood clotting, but its cousin, vitamin K_2, is not as well known. This vitamin is needed for a host of newly discovered functions in the human body, including working in synergy with vitamin D to calcify bone and prevent calcification of other organs.[14] Some experts are not satisfied with current vitamin K intakes of the US population.[15]

Meat and hard, fermented cheese, such as cheddar and parmesan, contain vitamin K_2. If there is sufficient "good" bacteria in the intestine—if they have not been killed by antibiotics—they convert vitamin K_1 to K_2.

Another form of vitamin K_2 has longer-lasting benefits and is found in nattō, a fermented soybean food eaten in Japan. Nattō has very large amounts of vitamin K_2, about 800 mcg per 100 g of nattō. However, nattō is an acquired taste.

> Vitamin K_2 is needed for a host of newly discovered functions in the human body, including working in synergy with vitamin D to calcify bone and prevent calcification of other organs.

I recommend a supplement with at least 80 mcg vitamin K_2, which is the recommended daily allowance.

Supplements

Eating a healthy diet that contains sufficient quantities of magnesium, zinc, boron, and vitamin K_2 is preferable to taking supplements, but to correct a deficiency (especially if your child is a picky eater), I recommend that autistic children take D_3Plus, which is available online.

Three capsules supply 5,000 IU of vitamin D_3, 225 mg magnesium, 3 mg boron, 12 mg zinc, and 80 mcg K_2. If your child takes more than 5,000 IU/day of vitamin D and needs more than three capsules, she takes in more of the other ingredients as well.

If your child takes D_3Plus and gets diarrhea (from the extra magnesium), reduce the D_3Plus intake and add regular vitamin D_3 capsules or drops to arrive at the required units of vitamin D.

If the child cannot swallow capsules, cut open the D_3Plus capsules with scissors and dissolve the contents in a smoothie.

GENERAL DIET TIPS

Autistic children are notoriously fussy eaters, so it is difficult for some of them to consume a good diet. Parents should not go overboard in trying to get a child to eat well. A knock-down drag-out fight benefits no one, especially since we know who will win.

Sometimes it is better to lead by example. Make a great-tasting smoothie with fruits and vegetables and put it on the counter next to you when feeding your child. Without being obvious, take sips of it occasionally and show the child you like it, again without being too obvious. If the child shows interest, offer him a small spoon with some of the smoothie, but make it clear that it is yours and you want the rest for yourself. With a little luck, and if you play your cards right, you may get him to drink a vegetable/fruit smoothie in a few days.

Lots of colorful fruits and vegetables (a "rainbow diet") should be at the core of your child's diet. Although not often discussed, potassium is one reason experts tell us to eat fruits and vegetables every day. There is no literature on potassium deficiency in autism, but you can estimate potassium intake from the vegetables and fruits in the child's diet. The child should eat a healthy and varied diet that contains fruits and some green, leafy vegetables.

It is difficult to get adequate potassium without eating four to six servings of fruit and vegetables each day. If your child will not eat vegetables, try a vegetable juice, even one mixed with fruit juices—anything to get some vegetables in her.

If old enough, the child should eat whole grains, seeds, and nuts (especially tree nuts such as walnuts, pecans, and almonds) or their butters if the child is too young for whole nuts.

Again, a bowl of dried fruit and nuts on the table may interest a child once she sees others in the family eating them.

In addition, varied sources of protein, such as meat, fish, eggs, and dairy products (if they are allowed), are important.

If your child doesn't or can't eat dairy products, he or she will most likely need a calcium supplement—at least 250–500 mg per day, depending on age and weight. With high-dose vitamin D, calcium, magnesium, and boron are very important, or calcium leaches from your child's bones to supply the body's other needs. Yogurt several times a day is a reasonable way to give your child some of the needed calcium.

> Researchers at Harvard believe that intestinal and food allergy problems may also be improved with vitamin D.

Researchers at Harvard believe that the intestinal and food allergy problems so common in modern children, such as milk allergy, may also be improved with vitamin D, which promotes a general, healthy barrier function (preventing bad things from getting inside; organs with a barrier function include the intestine, skin, lungs, and nose).[16] Food allergies and intolerance are increasing among children, right along with the epidemic of vitamin D deficiency. Vitamin D is involved in barrier functions throughout the body.[17] Gastrointestinal problems are more common in autism.[18] There is evidence that these problems are related to impaired gastrointestinal barrier functions.[19]

The child also needs red meat for iron and cold-water fatty fish, such as salmon and sardines, for omega-3 fatty acids. If the child will not eat fish, or if you are vegetarian or vegan, try omega-3 supplements. At least one randomized controlled trial of omega-3 supplements has been shown to help in ASD.[20]

Eggs are a traditional food for children and contain not only needed protein but other nutrients as well.

IN CONCLUSION

Here is the bottom line for your autistic child:

- Give adequate doses of vitamin D_3.
- Make sure your child is getting adequate amounts of magnesium, zinc, boron, and vitamin K_2.
- Do not give your child cod liver oil or preformed retinol vitamin A, such as retinyl acetate or retinyl palmitate, either by itself or in multivitamins.
- Calcium supplements (250–500 mg/day, depending on weight) are important if your child does not eat dairy products three times daily.

CHAPTER ELEVEN

WHAT WE NEED NOW

My theory of vitamin D may indeed explain part of the epidemic of autism, but it is not enough to understand the entire problem. We—people with autism, parents, parents-to-be, doctors, scientists, and the government—need to take action. First, predisposing factors and effective treatments for autism need to be established and confirmed through further study; to do that, scientists must have funding opportunities from large government agencies such as the National Institutes of Health. Unfortunately, the wheels of science turn very slowly, and it could take years or even decades to establish a convincing body of evidence.

The good news is that people with autism, parents, parents-to-be, and doctors don't have to wait for this to happen. We can take action right now, because part of what we need is available on the Internet and on grocery store shelves. Even if vitamin D turns out to be only part of the solution, it can only help and can't hurt.

PARENTS AND PEOPLE WITH AUTISM

Exposure to the sun is vital for people with autism because it does more than just provide vitamin D, but sunshine alone seldom raises vitamin D levels to the high-normal range. To do this, vitamin D_3 supplements are needed. Most American labs list normal calcidiol levels as 30–100 ng/mL, so the goal of treatment is to raise levels to 80 ng/mL. Some labs use different testing methods and list normal ranges as 20–75 ng/mL. In such cases, try to obtain levels of about 65 ng/mL.

The main problem with such advice is that parents soon learn that it takes adult doses of vitamin D (5,000–15,000 IU daily) to effectively obtain such levels in autistic children—sometimes more, especially in obese or older children. Parents are understandably concerned about using adult dosages. However, with vitamin D, blood level

> Until we know more, if you want your child to obtain optimum benefits, you should probably use both sunlight and supplements.

dictates dosage, so if your child's vitamin D levels are high-normal, your dosage is correct. The higher the dosage, the more often you should check calcidiol levels because adequacy of dose and safety are the major concerns.

The brand of vitamin D supplements I recommend is BioTech Pharmacal's D_3Plus; for younger children who can't swallow capsules, just dissolve the contents of the capsules in a smoothie. If it takes 10,000 IU/day to raise calcidiol levels to 80 ng/mL, then 10,000 IU/day is the correct dosage.

What happens if the blood level exceeds 100 ng/mL? Usually, nothing at all. It is called hypervitaminosis D. True vitamin D toxicity classically begins when vitamin D levels exceed 200 ng/mL and blood calcium is also elevated. You must have both lab abnormalities to have "toxicity." Levels between 100 and 150 ng/mL (hypervitaminosis D) are safe in the short term as long as the blood calcium level is normal and the dosage of vitamin D is promptly decreased.

Mild high blood calcium is dangerous only if it goes undetected for many months or years. Even then, the chance of it causing permanent kidney damage is quite small if the dose is reduced.

Until we know more, if you want your child to obtain optimum benefits, you should probably use both sunlight and supplements. Exposing the body to sunlight simply replicates one of the conditions present when humans first became humans, before autism became epidemic. So to me, that seems like the conservative thing to do.

In northern areas, sunbathe your child in the spring and summer and also use supplements; in the fall and winter, use vitamin D supplements only. In southern areas, sunbathe and also give supplements year around. Remember never to sunburn, because sunlight tends to damage the skin if you stay out too long.

PARENTS-TO-BE

Both parents need to sunbathe and take 5,000 IU of vitamin D per day before conceiving. (By the way, vitamin D appears to improve both male and female fertility.[1]) When the woman becomes pregnant, she should continue sunbathing and take 6,000 IU/day: 5,000 for her and 1,000 for the fetus.

After the child is born, give him or her 1,000 IU/day until he or she weighs 25 pounds, then increase the dose to 2,000 IU/day. If the mother is breastfeeding, she should take 6,000 IU/day, and she does not need to supplement the infant. Infants and toddlers should not avoid sunshine, only sunburns.

DOCTORS

Of all the studies I have referenced in this book, few are as upsetting as the CDC's 2010 study in the influential journal *Pediatrics*.[2] Cria Perrine and her colleagues at the CDC concluded that very few infants are getting the AAP-recommended intake of 400 IU/day. They found that the use of oral vitamin D supplements in the United States is very low. Among infants who consumed breast milk but no formula, only 13 percent met the AAP recommendation; among mixed-fed infants, only 14 percent met the AAP vitamin D recommendation; and among infants who consumed only formula, only 37 percent met the recommended intakes.

The authors concluded, "Our findings suggest that most US infants are not consuming adequate amounts of vitamin D, according to the 2008 recommendation. Pediatricians and healthcare providers should encourage parents of infants who are either breastfed or consuming less than 1 L/day of infant formula to give their infants an oral vitamin D supplement." This means that pediatricians are not telling the parents of these infants to follow this recommendation. Although I think 400 IU/day is too little, it is a lot better than what most infants are getting, which is much less. So, one thing that needs to change is to ensure that pediatricians begin following their own organization's recommendation.

GOVERNMENT

The US government sets adequate intakes of vitamin D through the Institute of Medicine's Food and Nutrition Board, which last met in 2010. A lot of research has been completed since then, much of it showing a clear benefit to doses higher than the 2010 recommendations. Scientists have published more than 12,000 vitamin D studies since 2010. (The board will meet again in about 2020 because it will want to review the large randomized controlled trial results, and the major ones are due to be completed by 2020.)

Government agencies must also make autism research more of a priority when issuing funding opportunities for scientists. Although there are many topics worthy of research, and funding is scarce, this is an epidemic, and I believe the health and well-being of children should be a national priority.

Scientists

Randomized controlled trials of vitamin D in both prevention and treatment are urgently needed, but they cost money—money that few institutions have. When the findings are positive, the researchers must use high doses of vitamin D in autistic children: at least 5,000 IU/day. Usually, open-label studies precede randomized controlled trials and, to date, only one open-label trial has been done. It showed that 5,000 IU/day helped 80 percent of autistic children.[3] Another open-label trial (funded by the Vitamin D Council) at the University of California, San Francisco, is still recruiting research subjects.[4]

A host of epidemiological studies could be done: autism and latitude, autism and sun exposure, vitamin D levels and severity of autism, sunscreen use in pregnant women and autism, sunscreen use in toddlers and autism, calcidiol and levels of brain-damaging antibodies in autism, just to name a few.

A study that could be easily done with existing data includes analyzing vitamin D intake data in infants to see if autistic children were less likely to receive vitamin D supplements or sun exposure as an infant than typically developing children. Because so few American infants are getting sun exposure or the AAP-recommended amount of vitamin D, it might be difficult to identify enough infants to follow over time.

What about toddlers? Are they getting enough sun exposure? Did toddlers who developed autism have less sun exposure, more sunscreen use, or less vitamin D supplementation than typically developing toddlers? This would be another fruitful avenue of research.

Genetic studies are also needed. What are levels of inherited vitamin D enzymes in autism? Are any vitamin D small genetic differences in enzymes (catalysts that speed up the body's conversion of vitamin D for use) associated with autism? Are the numerous small de novo mutations seen in autism a cause or an effect?

We also need scientists to study autism prevalence trends in different countries; the effect of diet as a risk factor and how it affects symptoms; and the link between acetaminophen use and autism risk. Also, do people with autism have a greater risk of other diseases such as respiratory tract infections, multiple sclerosis, and osteoporosis? In addition, it is very important to know at which stage of fetal development or infancy/early childhood the vitamin D injury occurs; is it gestational, or does it occur in early toddlerhood?

Do those with autism always show evidence of development problems as a fetus? What factors determine where a person falls on the autism spectrum (mild or severe)? Also, in one study, gestation during the winter months was associated with an over-representation of children with autism in a group of children born at the same time in the United Kingdom.[5] There was also an association between autism and spring births.[6] Both of these studies need to be repeated.

IN CONCLUSION

There is convincing evidence that vitamin D is involved in autism. I have reviewed most of that evidence in this book: everything from epidemiological studies to test-tube studies to animal studies and some human studies. It will be years, maybe decades, before the needed research is done. Parents must decide what to do in the meantime. Almost every decision made in medicine and in life is a risk/benefit analysis, just as when you take an aspirin tablet or get into your car. The doctor or the parent must balance the potential benefits of an action against the potential risks.

With respect to vitamin D and autism, the risk of using high physiological doses of vitamin D and sunbathing is minuscule if frequent vitamin D blood tests are done. The potential benefits, however, are enormous.

GLOSSARY

24-hydroxylase: Enzyme that breaks down vitamin D in the body.

Activated vitamin D: Biologically active form of vitamin D.

Albinism: Genetic condition in which the body can't produce or distribute melanin, a natural substance that gives color to your hair, skin, and iris, resulting in white skin and hair and pinkish irises.

Antibodies: Proteins produced by the body's immune system when it detects antigens (harmful substances that can lead to illness). Antibodies are helpful; however, when the immune system accidentally considers healthy body tissue a harmful substance, antibodies can damage healthy tissue. When this occurs, it is called an autoimmune disease.

Antidote: Type of medicine used to counteract, or stop, the effects of a toxin.

Antimicrobial peptides: Naturally occurring antibiotics in the lungs, respiratory tract, immune cells, intestines, and skin.

Atherosclerosis: A buildup of cholesterol in the arteries that can lead to blockage.

ATP (adenosine triphosphate): High-energy molecule that stores energy in each cell of the body.

Basal cell carcinoma: Type of non-melanoma skin cancer.

Beriberi: Illness brought on by a lack of vitamin B_1 (thiamine) in the diet.

Biomarker: Measure of a substance's (usually a hormone) effect on the body.

Biopsy: Sample of tissue taken from the body to examine it more closely.

Blinded: Pertaining to an experiment or clinical trial in which the researchers but not the subjects know which subjects are receiving the intervention or placebo.

Broad autism phenotype: Form of autism that occurs disproportionately in the parents of a child with autism, indicating a genetic factor. It is not a diagnosis as much as the recognition of observable traits similar to those found in someone with autism spectrum disorder.

Calcidiol: Also known as 25-hydroxyvitamin D, or 25(OH)D, calcidiol is a prehormone produced in the liver when an enzyme converts vitamin D_3 into a usable form of vitamin D_3 by an enzyme. Calcidiol is measured by physicians to determine vitamin D status.

Calcitriol: Steroid hormone whose building block is vitamin D.

Carcinogen: Cancer-causing agent.

Cathelicidin: Antimicrobial peptide that kills harmful viruses, bacteria, and fungi.

Chelate: To capture and excrete (used here in terms of heavy metals).

Chemotherapy: Use of drugs to treat cancer.

Cholesterol: Fat-like substance that can be found in every cell of the body. It is also found in many foods.

Chromosome: Package that holds DNA, which is the set of genetic instructions used in all living organisms.

Cortical thinness: The cortex is the straw-like part of the bone that indicates bone growth. Cortical thinness is often observed in children with autism.

Cortisone: Steroid hormone released by the adrenal gland in response to stress.

Dementia: General term for a decline in mental ability that interferes with activities of daily living.

De novo: Occurring for the first time.

DNA (deoxyribonucleic acid): Molecule that contains a complete set of genetic instructions for the formation and function of all living organisms.

Down syndrome: Also known as trisomy 21, it is a genetic disorder caused by a third copy of chromosome 21.

Endorphins: Naturally produced morphine-like molecules that are produced with exercise and other activities.

Epidemic: Widespread occurrence of an infectious disease in a particular area at a particular time.

Enzyme: Catalyst, or substance, that activates, speeds up, or slows down a biological process.

Epigenetics: The study of heritable (passed down from parent to child) changes in gene activity not caused by DNA sequence changes.

Expressed: A gene is expressed when its genotype gives rise to the phenotype (e.g., when a gene for green eyes shows up as green eyes in the offspring).

Facial recognition: Ability to remember faces by mentally comparing them to a "face library" of people you've met before.

False memory syndrome: A condition in which a person's identity and relationships are affected by memories of events that never happened but are strongly believed.

Folic acid: Also called folate, it is a form of water-soluble vitamin B_9 that is important in preventing birth defects.

Fragile X syndrome: Genetic disease that causes a spectrum of developmental issues ranging from learning disabilities to cognitive impairment.

Genetic: Resulting from a trait (gene) passed from generation to generation. For example, if your father had a cleft chin and you have one, too, you likely inherited that trait from him and may pass it on to your own child.

Genotype: Genetic makeup of a cell.

Gestation: Time during pregnancy in which an embryo develops into a fetus.

Glutathione: Important antioxidant that protects cells from damage from free radicals.

Hereditability: The amount a specific trait is controlled by inheritance from the parents to the offspring.

Hypercalcemia: High levels of calcium in the blood.

Hypercalcuria: High levels of calcium in the urine.

Hyperparathyroidism: Condition characterized by having too much parathyroid hormone in the bloodstream due to overactivity of one or more of the body's four parathyroid glands in the neck.

Hypervitaminosis D: Condition characterized by abnormally high (but not toxic) levels of vitamin D.

Hypothesis: Proposed explanation for a phenomenon such as a disease.

Immunological triggers: Foreign substance that produces an immune response.

Internal cancers: Cancers of organs, blood, or tissues inside the body.

Ionizing radiation: Particularly damaging form of radiation that can break chemical bonds in the body, creating highly reactive ions (particles with an electrical charge).

IU (International Unit): Unit of measurement for some vitamins. We use IUs to acknowledge that all batches of the same vitamin may not have the same mass, but they perform the same activities in the body.

Lactose intolerance: Inability to digest the sugar lactose, which is found in dairy products.

Lesion: Any abnormality in tissues such as skin.

Lethal: Deadly.

Lupus: Long-term autoimmune disease that damages different parts of the body.

Lymph nodes: Small, bean-shaped glands found throughout the body; part of the lymph system.

Lymphoma: Blood cell tumors.

Mechanism: In medicine, the pathogenesis, or development, of a disease.

Melanoma: The most dangerous form of skin cancer, melanoma occurs when DNA damage to skin cells, mostly due to ultraviolet radiation from the sun or tanning booths, trigger genetic defects that cause the skin cells to multiply rapidly and form cancerous tumors.

Metastatic: Cancer that has spread; no longer localized.

Mitochondrial theory of autism: The theory that autism is caused by dysfunction of the mitochondria, membrane-bound organelles that act as the "powerhouses" of the cell.

Mole: Brown or black growths on the skin that can be noncancerous or cancerous.

Multiple sclerosis: Disabling autoimmune disease in which the body's immune system attacks the body's protective nerve covering, interfering with the body's ability to communicate with the brain, spinal cord, and other parts of the body. The nerves themselves may also deteriorate.

Neurotrophins: Proteins that help neurons survive, develop, and function.

Niacin: Vitamin B_3.

Nucleic acids: Large biological molecules that are the building blocks of all life.

Obsessive-compulsive disorder (OCD): Anxiety disorder characterized by unwanted, recurring thoughts that produce fear or uneasiness. In order to control the fear, the person with OCD engages in repetitive behaviors, such as hand washing or checking to make sure the doors are locked.

Osteomalacia: Bone-softening condition that is often due to lack of vitamin D.

Osteoporosis: Disease that leads to weakened, brittle bones, often associated with aging and insufficient intake of calcium and vitamin D.

Palmitate: Preformed vitamin A in pill form.

Parathyroid hormone: Most common biomarker for measuring vitamin D levels.

Parroting: Repeating in a robotic tone what was said.

Parsimony: The principle that the best theory is the one that can explain the most facts in the simplest manner.

Pathology: The study of disease and the change it causes.

Pellagra: Disease caused by vitamin B_3 (niacin) deficiency.

Peptide: Naturally occurring antibiotic in the lungs, respiratory tract, immune cells, intestines, and skin.

Phenotype: All of a person's observable characteristics (from a combination of genetics and the environment). Examples include body shape and size, behaviors, and personality traits.

Photosensitivity dermatitis: Rash most often caused by exposure to sunlight.

Pineal gland: Pea-size organ in the middle of the brain.

Placebo: "Sugar pill," or inactive substance, given to some subjects as part of a scientific study.

Point mutations: Small alteration in the genetic code occurring at a single point on the DNA.

Polymorphous light eruption: Itchy rash that occurs in response to exposure to sunlight in people who have developed a sensitivity to it.

Porphyria: Disorders that result from a buildup of natural chemicals that produce porphyrin, which is essential for the proper function of hemoglobin, in the body. High levels of porphyrins can lead to different types of problems throughout the body.

Precursors: Things that precede something else.

Preformed vitamin A: Pill form of vitamin A consisting of retinyl acetate and palmitate. Retinyl is converted to retinoic acid, the form of vitamin A that affects gene transcription.

Prehormone: Substance with minimal or no significant biological activity until it is converted into an active hormone.

Pre-vitamin D: Intermediate form in the production of vitamin D.

Prostate: Gland in the male reproductive system that secretes a milky fluid that makes up as much as 75 percent of the fluid in semen.

Protein allergy: Reaction caused by a particular protein found in a particular food.

Radon: Naturally occurring, colorless, odorless, tasteless gas that is known to cause lung cancer.

Retina: Light-sensitive layer of tissue lining the inner surface of the eye.

Retinyl acetate: Preformed vitamin A in pill form.

Recovered memory therapy: Discredited form of psychotherapy based on the belief that mental illnesses such as depression and anxiety are caused by repressed memories of childhood sexual abuse. It is based on the assumption that the patient can reclaim mental health only by facing these memories.

Replicating: Process of a cell making copies of itself.

Rickets: Bone-softening disease caused by a lack of vitamin D.

Sarcoidosis: Disease that causes inflammation. It can affect any organ in the body.

Schizophrenia: Disabling, chronic, serious mental illness characterized by psychosis and paranoia.

Secondary hyperparathyroidism: Elevated levels of parathyroid hormone in the blood caused by low vitamin D levels.

Serum: Clear bodily fluid from which all clotting proteins in the blood have been removed.

Social anxiety: Also known as social phobia, this is a type of chronic (long-term) yet treatable anxiety that may include intense fear of talking with strangers, worry that you are being judged or that you are humiliating yourself, concern that others will notice your anxiety, avoidance of situations in which you might be the center of attention, blushing, sweating heavily, or trembling or shaking, or nausea.

Solar zenith angle: Altitude of the sun in the sky.

Spina bifida: Genetic disorder characterized by the incomplete closing of the neural tube.

Squamous cell carcinoma: Type of non-melanoma skin cancer.

Steroid hormone: Steroid that acts as a hormone.

SPF: Sun protection factor rating for sunscreen. For example, an SPF of 20 allows you, in theory, to stay in the sun 20 times longer than without sunscreen. That is, if you normally burn in 10 minutes, you could stay in the sun for 3 hours and 20 minutes without reapplying the sunscreen.

Sunscreen: A chemical-based lotion, spray, or gel applied to the skin to absorb or reflect some of the sun's ultraviolet radiation on the skin and help protect against sunburn, skin cancer, and the aging effects of the sun.

Thiamine: Vitamin B_1.

Toxemia: Sudden rise in blood pressure in a pregnant woman. Commonly called pre-eclampsia.

Toxicity: Poisoning, or the degree to which a substance can damage tissues, organs, or the entire body.

Toxicology: Branch of biology concerned with identifying the effect of different toxins on the body.

Transcription: Gene activity using the DNA message to produce RNA, which then produces the proteins and enzymes needed for life.

T regulatory cells (tregs): Subgroup of T-cells that modulate the immune system.

Tuberculosis: Common and often deadly infectious disease of the lungs.

Ultraviolet radiation: Potentially damaging radiation in sunlight.

Up-regulating: Increasing.

Vitamin D_2: Also called ergocalciferol, it is a much less potent form of circulating vitamin D_3 (cholecalciferol). It also has a shorter duration of action.

Vitamin D_3: Also called cholecalciferol, it is a much more potent form of circulating vitamin D than vitamin D_2 (ergocalciferol). It also has a longer duration of action.

Vitamin D–binding protein: Protein encoded by a gene that carries vitamin D to the liver.

Vitamin D hypersensitivity: Sensitivity to vitamin D (any amount) in people with certain diseases that are a risk factor for hypercalcemia (too much calcium in the blood). One example is the disease sarcoidosis.

Vitamin D response element: DNA sequence in the promoter region of vitamin D–regulated genes.

Valproic acid: Mood-stabilizing, anti-seizure drug.

Water intoxication: Also called hyponatremia (low blood sodium), it is a deadly condition caused by consuming too much water, which dilutes the electrolytes in the blood to dangerously low levels.

Williams syndrome: Rare genetic syndrome, known as the "Un-Autistic Syndrome," in which fetuses and very young infants have exceptionally high blood levels of activated vitamin D. Children with Williams syndrome have outgoing personalities, perhaps because their brains were flooded with vitamin D during certain stages of brain development.

Zinc oxide: White, powdered chemical often used in sunscreens to protect the skin against the ultraviolet rays of the sun.

ABOUT THE VITAMIN D COUNCIL

After I realized that vitamin D deficiency was so widespread and that vitamin D was crucial to health, I created a nonprofit, tax-exempt, 501(c)(3) organization dedicated to educating both professionals and the public about the dangers of vitamin D deficiency. I first wrote about the vitamin D theory of autism with the Vitamin D Council. In fact, I wrote about vitamin D and autism in the council's newsletter a full year before I published my theory in *Medical Hypotheses* in 2007.

Visit the Vitamin D Council's website, vitamindcouncil.org, where you can learn more about vitamin D. Four million unique users have used the website each year. You can make a tax-free donation or become a member of the council (also tax-free) for $5 per month. Members have access to all content on the website, including my frequent blog posts.

In addition to the website, the Vitamin D Council provides free information to both professionals and the public through a newsletter about the latest vitamin D research. Newsletter subscribers can learn about vitamin D breakthroughs before most physicians and other health professionals do. The website also offers practical advice on how to prevent vitamin D deficiency and insights into the world of vitamin D research, including its relationship with autism.

The Vitamin D Council has funded a clinical study using vitamin D to treat autism, which is currently recruiting study subjects at the University of California at San Francisco.

In this book, I recommend a vitamin D formulation that I designed, D_3Plus, which is manufactured by BioTech Pharmacal. I also recommend in-home blood tests for parents. Both D_3Plus and in-home vitamin D blood testing are available on the Vitamin D Council's website; the council makes $1 for every bottle of D_3Plus sold and $10 for every vitamin D blood test kit sold.

The Vitamin D Council has not yet secured a grant to fund operations. Instead, it relies on membership subscriptions, sales of in-home vitamin D blood tests, sales of D_3Plus, and donations from sponsors—but mostly charitable contributions from the public. Should the information in this book prove helpful to you and your family, I would appreciate it very much if you made a tax-deductible charitable contribution through the Vitamin D Council website.

ABOUT THE AUTHOR

John J. Cannell, MD, graduated Phi Beta Kappa from the University of Maryland in 1972 with a degree in zoology. He earned his medical degree from the University of North Carolina at Chapel Hill in 1976 and his board certification in psychiatry and neurology in 1993.

In 2003, he founded a nonprofit corporation, the Vitamin D Council, to educate physicians and the public about the importance of vitamin D in health. Dr. Cannell has authored the book *Athlete's Edge: Faster Quicker Stronger with Vitamin D*; written or coauthored 27 scientific articles in peer-reviewed journals; and given presentations at numerous conferences, including the 92nd Annual Meeting of the American Association for the Advancement of Science, Pacific Division. He is a member of the American Medical Association. Several of his efforts to improve public health, healthcare, and public education have received national media coverage.

Currently, Dr. Cannell is executive director of the Vitamin D Council, Inc.; president and treasurer of Cannell Nutrition, Inc.; principal and practicing physician at San Luis Obispo Integrative Medicine; and on the scientific advisory board for Opko Health, Inc. (consulting about the treatment of autism). He lives in San Luis Obispo, California.

ACKNOWLEDGMENT

I would like to thank Mary Van Beusekom, ELS, of Synapse Writing & Editing, for her competency, thoroughness, and professionalism.

REFERENCES

Dedication

[1] McGrath J, Feron F, Eyles D, Mackay-Sim A. Vitamin D: the neglected neurosteroid? Trends Neurosci. 2001;24(10):570-572.

Foreword

[1] Centers for Disease Control and Prevention, Developmental Disabilities Monitoring Network Surveillance Year 2010 Principal Investigators; Centers for Disease Control and Prevention. Prevalence of autism spectrum disorder among children aged 8 years—Autism and Developmental Disabilities Monitoring Network, 11 sites, United States, 2010. MMWR Surveill Summ. 2014;28;63(2):1-21.

[2] Buescher AV, Cidav Z, Knapp M, Mandell DS. Costs of autism spectrum disorders in the United Kingdom and the United States. JAMA Pediatr. 2014;168(8):721-728. doi: 10.1001/jamapediatrics.2014.210. [Epub ahead of print.]

[3] McGrath J. Hypothesis: Is low prenatal vitamin D a risk-modifying factor for schizophrenia? Schizophr Res. 1999;40(3):173-177.

[4] McGrath J. Does 'imprinting' with low prenatal vitamin D contribute to the risk of various adult disorders? Med Hypotheses. 2001;56(3):367-371.

[5] Eyles D, Brown J, Mackay-Sim A, McGrath J, Feron F. Vitamin D_3 and brain development. Neuroscience. 2003;118(3):641-653.

[6] Cannell JJ, Vieth R, Umhau JC, Holick MF, Grant WB, Madronich S, et al. Epidemic influenza and vitamin D. Epidemiol Infect. 2006;134(6):1129-1140.

[7] Cannell JJ. Autism and vitamin D. Med Hypotheses. 2008;70(4):750-759.

[8] Skaaby T, Husemoen LL, Thuesen BH, Pisinger C, Jørgensen T, Roswall N, et al. Prospective population-based study of the association between serum 25-hydroxyvitamin-D levels and the incidence of specific types of cancer. Cancer Epidemiol Biomarkers Prev. 2014;23(7):1220-1229.

[9] Grant WB, Cannell JJ. Autism prevalence in the United States with respect to solar ultraviolet-B doses: An ecological study. Dermatoendocrinol. 2013;5(1):159-164.

[10] Hill AB. The environment and disease: Association or causation? Proc R Soc Med. 1965;58:295-300.

Preface

[1] Patrick RP, Ames BN. Vitamin D hormone regulates serotonin synthesis. Part 1: relevance for autism. FASEB J. 2014;28(6):2398-2413. Epub 2014 Feb 20.

[2] Kočovská E, Andorsdóttir G, Weihe P, Halling J, Fernell E, Stóra T, et al. Vitamin D in the general population of young adults with autism in the Faroe Islands. J Autism Dev Disord. 2014 Jun 14. [Epub ahead of print].

[3] Saad K, et al. Vitamin D status in autism spectrum disorder and the efficacy of vitamin D supplementation in autistic children. Submitted for publication.

[4] King BH, Dukes K, Donnelly CL, Sikich L, McCracken JT, Scahill L, et al. Baseline factors predicting placebo response to treatment in children and adolescents with autism spectrum disorders: a multisite randomized clinical trial. JAMA Pediatr. 2013;167(11):1045-1052.

Introduction

[1] Prevalence of autism spectrum disorder among children aged 8 years—autism and developmental disabilities monitoring network, 11 sites, United States, 2010. Developmental Disabilities Monitoring Network Surveillance Year 2010 Principal Investigators; Centers for Disease Control and Prevention (CDC). MMWR Surveill Summ. 2014;63(2):1-21.

[2] Autism and Developmental Disabilities Monitoring Network Surveillance Year 2008 Principal Investigators; Centers for Disease Control and Prevention. Prevalence of autism spectrum disorders—Autism and Developmental Disabilities Monitoring Network, 14 sites, United States, 2008. MMWR Surveill Summ. 2012;61(3):1-19.

[3] Ganz ML. The lifetime distribution of the incremental societal costs of autism. Arch Pediatr Adolesc Med 2007;161(4):343-349.

[4] Karst JS, Van Hecke AV. Parent and family impact of autism spectrum disorders: a review and proposed model for intervention evaluation. Clin Child Fam Psychol Rev. 2012;15(3):247-277.

[5] Hartley SL, Barker ET, Seltzer MM, Floyd F, Greenberg J, Orsmond G, et al. The relative risk and timing of divorce in families of children with an autism spectrum disorder. J Fam Psychol. 2010;24(4):449-457.

[6] Bouma R, Schweitzer R. The impact of chronic childhood illness on family stress: a comparison between autism and cystic fibrosis. J Clin Psychol. 1990;46(6):722-730.

[7] Cannell JJ. Autism and vitamin D. Med Hypotheses. 2008;70(4):750-759. Epub 2007 Oct 24.

[8] Deans E. Autism and vitamin D. The sun is not the enemy. Psych Today. 2011. Available at: http://www.psychologytoday.com/blog/evolutionary-psychiatry/201104/autism-and-vitamin-d. Accessed June 5, 2014.

[9] Glaser G. What if vitamin D deficiency is a cause of autism? Sci Amer. 2009. Available at: http://www.scientificamerican.com/article.cfm?id=vitamin-d-and-autism. Accessed June 5, 2014.

[10] Kinney DK, Barch DH, Chayka B, Napoleon S, Munir KM. Environmental risk factors for autism: do they help cause de novo genetic mutations that contribute to the disorder? Med Hypotheses. 2010;74(1):102-106. Epub 2009 Aug 21.

[11] Billstedt E, Gillberg IC, Gillberg C. Autism after adolescence: population-based 13- to 22-year follow-up study of 120 individuals with autism diagnosed in childhood. J Autism Dev Disord. 2005;35(3):351-360.

[12] Mostafa GA, AL-Ayadhi LY. Reduced serum concentrations of 25-hydroxy vitamin D in children with autism: Relation to autoimmunity. J Neuroinflammation. 2012;17(9):201. doi:10.1186/1742-2094-9-201.

Introduction Sidebar
[1] Losh M, Childress D, Lam K, Piven J. Defining key features of the broad autism phenotype: a comparison across parents of multiple- and single-incidence autism families. Am J Med Genet B Neuropsychiatr Genet. 2008;147B(4):424-433.

[2] Altman LK. The Doctor's World; One Physician Takes a Novel Stand Against Patients Who Smoke. February 9, 1988. The New York Times. Available at: http://www.nytimes.com/1988/02/09/science/the-doctor-s-world-one-physician-takes-a-novel-stand-against-patients-who-smoke.html. Accessed April 4, 2014.

[3] 60 Minutes. Teacher is a cheater. Available at: http://www.youtube.com/watch?v=jVloV2u14SQ. Accessed April 4, 2014.

[4] Cannell J, Hudson JI, Pope HG Jr. Standards for informed consent in recovered memory therapy. J Am Acad Psychiatry Law. 2001;29(2):138-147. Review.

[5] National Institutes of Health. Vitamin D. Available at: http://ods.od.nih.gov/factsheets/VitaminD-QuickFacts/. Accessed April 4, 2014.

Chapter One
[1] Kanner L. Autistic disturbances of affective contact. Nervous Child 1943;2:217-250.

[2] Asperger H. Die "Autistischen Psychopathen im Kindesalter [Autistic psychopaths in childhood]" (German). Archiv für Psychiatrie und Nervenkrankheiten. 1944:117:76-136.

[3] Hollander E, Kolevzon A, Coyle JT. Textbook of Autism Spectrum Disorders. American Psychiatric Publishing Inc. Washington, DC, 2011.

[4] Charlot L, Abend S, Ravin P, Mastis K, Hunt A, Deutsch C. Non-psychiatric health problems among psychiatric inpatients with intellectual disabilities. J Intellect Disabil Res. 2011;55(2):199-209.

[5] Hediger ML, England LJ, Molloy CA, Yu KF, Manning-Courtney P, Mills JL. Reduced bone cortical thickness in boys with autism or autism spectrum disorder. J Autism Dev Disord. 2008;38(5):848-856.

[6] Hagberg H, Gressens P, Mallard C. Inflammation during fetal and neonatal life: Implications for neurologic and neuropsychiatric disease in children and adults. Ann Neurol. 2012;71(4):444-457. doi: 10.1002/ana.22620. Epub 2012 Feb 14.

[7] Fisch GS. Nosology and epidemiology in autism: Classification counts. Am J Med Genet C Semin Med Genet. 2012;160C(2):91-103. Epub 2012 Apr 12.

[8] Nassar N, Dixon G, Bourke J, Bower C, Glasson E, de Klerk N, Leonard H. Autism spectrum disorders in young children: effect of changes in diagnostic practices. Int J Epidemiol. 2009;38(5):1245-1254.

[9] Arizumi A. DSM-V: Changes in the definition of autism. Birmingham Examiner. April 2, 2012. Available at: http://www.examiner.com/article/dsm-v-changes-the-definition-of-autism. Accessed May 21, 2014.

[10] Duchan E, Patel DR. Epidemiology of autism spectrum disorders. Pediatr Clin North Am. 2012;59(1):27-43, ix-x.

[11] Adams JB, Audhya T, McDonough-Means S, Rubin RA, Quig D, Geis E, et al. Effect of a vitamin/mineral supplement on children and adults with autism. BMC Pediatr. 2011;11:111.

[12] Amminger GP, Berger GE, Schäfer MR, Klier C, Friedrich MH, Feucht M. Omega-3 fatty acids supplementation in children with autism: a double-blind randomized, placebo-controlled pilot study. Biol Psychiatry. 2007;61(4):551-553. Epub 2006 Aug 22.

[13] McPheeters ML, Warren Z, Sathe N, Bruzek JL, Krishnaswami S, Jerome RN. A systematic review of medical treatments for children with autism spectrum disorders. Pediatrics. 2011;127(5):e1312-1321. Epub 2011 April 4.

Chapter Two
[1] Hallmayer J, Cleveland S, Torres A, Phillips J, Cohen B, Torigoe T, et al. Genetic heritability and shared environmental factors among twin pairs with autism. Arch Gen Psychiatry. 2011;68(11):1095-1102. doi: 10.1001/archgenpsychiatry.2011.76.

[2] O'Roak BJ, Vives L, Girirajan S, Karakoc E, Krumm N, Coe BP, et al. Sporadic autism exomes reveal a highly interconnected protein network of de novo mutations. Nature. 2012;485(7397):246-250.

[3] Reichenberg A, Gross R, Weiser M, Bresnaham M, Silverman J, Harlap S, et al. Advancing paternal age and autism. Arch Gen Psychiatry. 2006;63(9):1026-1032.

[4] Miyake K, Hirasawa T, Koide T, Kubota T. Epigenetics in autism and other neurodevelopmental diseases. Adv Exp Med Biol. 2012;724:91-98.

[5] Hossein-Nezhad A, Holick MF. Optimize dietary intake of vitamin D: an epigenetic perspective. Curr Opin Clin Nutr Metab Care. 2012;15(6):567-579.

[6] Wikipedia. Andrew Wakefield. Available at: http://en.wikipedia.org/wiki/Andrew_Wakefield. Accessed May 22, 2014.

[7] Dyer C. Lancet retracts Wakefield's MMR paper. BMJ. 2010;340:c696.

[8] Velan B. Acceptance on the move: public reaction to shifting vaccination realities. Hum Vaccin. 2011;7(12):1261-1270.

[9] Hensley E, Briars L. Closer look at autism and the measles-mumps-rubella vaccine. J Am Pharm Assoc. 2010;50(6):736-741.

[10] Schultz ST. Does thimerosal or other mercury exposure increase the risk for autism? A review of current literature. Acta Neurobiol Exp (Wars). 2010;70(2):187-195.

[11] Gesundheit B, Rosenzweig JP, Naor D, Lerer B, Zachor DA, Procházka V, et al. Immunological and autoimmune considerations of autism spectrum disorders. J Autoimmun. 2013;44:1-7.

[12] Patterson PH. Immune involvement in schizophrenia and autism: Etiology, pathology, and animal models. Behav Brain Res. 2009;204(2):313-321.

[13] Guillot X, Semerano L, Saidenberg-Kermanac'h N, Falgarone G, Boissier MC. Vitamin D and inflammation. Joint Bone Spine. 2010;77:552-557.

[14] Abdallah MW, Larsen N, Grove J, Nørgaard-Petersen B, Thorsen P, Mortensen EL, et al. Amniotic fluid inflammatory cytokines: Potential markers of immunologic dysfunction in autism spectrum disorders. World J Biol Psychiatry. 2013;14(7):528-538.

[15] Patterson PH. Maternal infection and immune involvement in autism. Trends Mol Med. 2011;17(7):389-394.

[16] Mostafa GA, Al-Ayadhi LY. Increased serum levels of anti-ganglioside M1 autoantibodies in autistic children: relation to the disease severity. J Neuroinflammation. 2011;8:39.

[17] Kriegel MA, Manson JE, Costenbader KH. Does vitamin D affect risk of developing autoimmune disease?: A systematic review. Semin Arthritis Rheum. 2011;40(6):512-531.e8.

[18] Yang CY, Leung PS, Adamopoulos IE, Gershwin ME. The implication of vitamin D and autoimmunity: a comprehensive review. Clin Rev Allergy Immunol. 2013;45(2):217-226.

[19] Weissman JR, Kelley RI, Bauman ML, Cohen BH, Murray KF, Mitchell RL, et al. Mitochondrial disease in autism spectrum disorder patients: a cohort analysis. PLoS One. 2008;3(11):e3815.

[20] Marazziti D, Baroni S, Picchetti M, Landi P, Silvestri S, Vatteroni V, et al. Psychiatric disorders and mitochondrial dysfunctions. Eur Rev Med Pharmacol Sci. 2012;16(2):270-275.

[21] Lerman-Sagie T, Leshinsky-Silver E, Watemberg N, Lev D. Should autistic children be evaluated for mitochondrial disorders? J Child Neurol. 2004;19(5):379-381.

[22] Sinha A, Hollingsworth KG, Ball S, Cheetham T. Improving the vitamin D status of vitamin D deficient adults is associated with improved mitochondrial oxidative function in skeletal muscle. J Clin Endocrinol Metab. 2013;98(3):E509-E513.

[23] Kinney DK, Barch DH, Chayka B, Napoleon S, Munir KM. Environmental risk factors for autism: Do they help cause de novo genetic mutations that contribute to the disorder? Med Hypotheses. 2010;74(1):102-106.

[24] Top ten toxic chemicals suspected to cause autism and learning disabilities. Science Daily. April 25, 2012. Available at: http://www.sciencedaily.com/releases/2012/04/120425140118.htm. Accessed May 22, 2014.

[25] Lodish H, Berk A, Matsudaira P, Kaiser CA, Krieger M, Scott MP, et al. Molecular Biology of the Cell, 5th ed. p. 963. 2004. WH Freeman: New York, NY.

[26] Bianconi E, Piovesan A, Facchin F, Beraudi A, Casadei R, Frabetti F, et al. An estimation of the number of cells in the human body. Ann Hum Biol. 2013;40(6):463-471.

[27] Janusonis S. Serotonergic paradoxes of autism replicated in a simple mathematical model. Med Hypotheses. 2005;64(4):742-750.

[28] Patrick RP, Ames BN. Vitamin D hormone regulates serotonin synthesis. Part 1: relevance for autism. FASEB J. 2014;28(6):2398-2413. Epub 2014 Feb 20. Review.

Chapter Three

[1] Walton AG. Living Life with Autism: Has Anything Really Changed? Forbes. Nov 30, 2011.

[2] Autism and Developmental Disabilities Monitoring Network Surveillance Year 2008 Principal Investigators; Centers for Disease Control and Prevention. Prevalence of autism spectrum disorders—Autism and Developmental Disabilities Monitoring Network, 14 sites, United States, 2008. MMWR Surveill Summ. 2012;30;61(3):1-19.

[3] Cannell JJ. Autism and vitamin D. Med Hypotheses. 2008;70(4):750-759. Epub 2007 Oct 24.

[4] O'Roak BJ, Vives L, Girirajan S, Karakoc E, Krumm N, Coe BP, et al. Sporadic autism exomes reveal a highly interconnected protein network of de novo mutations. Nature. 2012;485:246-250. doi: 10.1038/nature10989. [Epub ahead of print]

[5] Cannell JJ. On the aetiology of autism. Acta Paediatr. 2010;99(8):1128-1130. Epub 2010 May 19.

[6] Holick MF. Vitamin D deficiency. N Engl J Med. 2007;357(3):266-81. Review.

[7] Council on Physical Therapy. Regulations to govern advertising of ultraviolet generators to the medical profession only. JAMA. 1925;98:400.

[8] Wright A. Immunity. Encyclopedia Britannica, 14th ed. 1929;12:117.

[9] U.S. Department of Labor, Children's Bureau, Sunlight for Babies. Folder No. 5 1931. Available at: http://www.mchlibrary.info/history/chbu/29412.pdf. Accessed June 8, 2014.

[10] Hawking, Stephen (2003). On the Shoulders of Giants. Running Press. p. 731. ISBN 0-7624-1698-X.

[11] Kalkbrenner AE, Daniels JL, Chen JC, Poole C, Emch M, Morrissey J. Perinatal exposure to hazardous air pollutants and autism spectrum disorders at age 8. Epidemiology. 2010;21(5):631-641.

[12] Windham GC, Zhang L, Gunier R, Croen LA, Grether JK. Autism spectrum disorders in relation to distribution of hazardous air pollutants in the San Francisco Bay area. Environ Health Perspect 2006;114(9):1438-1444.

[13] Waldman M, Nicholson S, Adilov N, Williams J. Autism prevalence and precipitation rates in California, Oregon, and Washington counties. Arch Pediatr Adolesc Med. 2008;162(11):1026-1034.

[14] Hediger ML, England LJ, Molloy CA, Yu KF, Manning-Courtney P, Mills JL. Reduced bone cortical thickness in boys with autism or autism spectrum disorder. J Autism Dev Disord. 2008;38(5):848-856.

[15] Durkin MS, Maenner MJ, Meaney FJ, Levy SE, DiGuiseppi C, Nicholas JS, et al. Socioeconomic inequality in the prevalence of autism spectrum disorder: evidence from a U.S. cross-sectional study. PLoS One. 2010;12;5(7):e11551.

[16] Bhasin TK, Schendel D. Sociodemographic risk factors for autism in a US metropolitan area. J Autism Dev Disord 2007;37(4):667-677.

[17] Croen LA, Grether JK, Hoogstrate J, Selvin S. The changing prevalence of autism in California. J Autism Dev Disord 2002;32(3):207-215.

[18] Hillman RE, Kanafani N, Takahashi TN, Miles JH. Prevalence of autism in Missouri: changing trends and the effect of a comprehensive state autism project. Mo Med 2000;97(5):159-163.

[19] Keen DV, Reid FD, Arnone D. Autism, ethnicity and maternal immigration. Br J Psychiatry. 2010;196(4):274-281.

[20] Goodman R, Richards H. Child and adolescent psychiatric presentations of second-generation Afro-Caribbeans in Britain. Br J Psychiatry 1995;167(3):362-369.

[21] Gillberg C, Schaumann H, Gillberg IC. Autism in immigrants: children born in Sweden to mothers born in Uganda. J Intellect Disabil Res 1995;39(Pt 2):141-144.

[22] Dealberto MJ. Prevalence of autism according to maternal immigrant

status and ethnic origin. Acta Psychiatr Scand. 2011;123(5):339-348. doi: 10.1111/j.1600-0447.2010.01662.x. Epub 2011 Jan 11.

23 Patrick RP, Ames BN. Vitamin D hormone regulates serotonin synthesis. Part 1: relevance for autism. FASEB J. 2014;28(6):2398-2413. Epub 2014 Feb 20.

24 Faurschou A, Beyer DM, Schmedes A, Bogh MK, Phillipsen PA, Wulf HC. The relation between sunscreen layer thickness and vitamin D production after UVB exposure—a randomized clinical trial. Br J Dermatol. 2012;167(2):391-395. doi: 10.1111/j.1365-2133.2012.11004.x.

25 Ultraviolet (UV) Radiation, Broad Spectrum and UVA, UVB, and UVC—National Toxicology Program. Ntp.niehs.nih.gov. 2009-01-05. Retrieved June 6, 2014.

26 Ginde AA, Liu MC, Camargo CA Jr. Demographic differences and trends of vitamin D insufficiency in the US population, 1988-2004. Arch Intern Med. 2009;169(6):626-632.

27 Skaaby T, Husemoen LL, Thuesen BH, Pisinger C, Jørgensen T, Roswall N, et al. Prospective population-based study of the association between serum 25-hydroxyvitamin-D levels and the incidence of specific types of cancer. Cancer Epidemiol Biomarkers Prev. 2014;23:1220-1229.

28 Grant WB. Why the prospective population-based study in Denmark did not find an association of 25-hydroxyvitamin D levels with cancer incidence rates, CEBP EPI-14-0530. Accepted June 2014.

29 Baïz N, Dargent-Molina P, Wark JD, Souberbielle JC, Slama R, Annesi-Maesano I; EDEN Mother-Child Cohort Study Group. Gestational exposure to urban air pollution related to a decrease in cord blood vitamin D levels. J Clin Endocrinol Metab. 2012;97(11):4087-4095.

30 Abrams SA, O'Brien KO. Calcium and bone mineral metabolism in children with chronic illnesses. Annu Rev Nutr. 2004;24:13-32.

31 Robinson JK, Rigel DS, Amonette RA. Summertime sun protection used by adults for their children. J Am Acad Dermatol 2000;42(5 Pt 1):746-753.

32 Hall HI, Jorgensen CM, McDavid K, Kraft JM, Breslow R. Protection from sun exposure in US white children ages 6 months to 11 years. Public Health Rep 2001;116(4):353-361.

33 Developmental Disabilities Monitoring Network Surveillance Year 2010 Principal Investigators; Centers for Disease Control and Prevention (CDC). Prevalence of autism spectrum disorder among children aged 8 years - Autism and Developmental Disabilities Monitoring Network, 11 sites, United States, 2010. MMWR Surveill Summ. 2014;63(2):1-21.

34 Bodnar LM, Simhan HN, Powers RW, Frank MP, Cooperstein E, Roberts JM. High prevalence of vitamin D insufficiency in black and white pregnant women residing in the northern United States and their neonates. J Nutr 2007;137(2):447-452.

[35] Kaplan P, Wang PP, Francke U. Williams (Williams Beuren) syndrome: a distinct neurobehavioral disorder. J Child Neurol 2001;16(3):177-190.

[36] Garabédian M, Jacqz E, Guillozo H, Grimberg R, Guillot M, Gagnadoux MF, et al. Elevated plasma 1,25-dihydroxyvitamin D concentrations in infants with hypercalcemia and an elfin facies. N Engl J Med 1985;312(15):948-952.

[37] Knudtzon J, Aksnes L, Akslen LA, Aarskog D. Elevated 1,25-dihydroxyvitamin D and normocalcaemia in presumed familial Williams syndrome. Clin Genet 1987;32(6):369-374.

[38] Mervis CB, Klein-Tasman BP. Williams syndrome: cognition, personality, and adaptive behavior. Ment Retard Dev Disabil Res Rev 2000;6(2):148-158.

Chapter Four

[1] Morris HA, Anderson PH. Autocrine and paracrine actions of vitamin D. Clin Biochem Rev. 2010;31(4):129-138.

[2] Holick MF. Vitamin D deficiency. N Engl J Med. 2007;357(3):266-281.

[3] Faurschou A, Beyer DM, Schmedes A, Bogh MK, Philipsen PA, Wulf HC. The relation between sunscreen layer thickness and vitamin D production after ultraviolet B exposure: a randomized clinical trial. Br J Dermatol. 2012;167(2):391-395. doi: 10.1111/j.1365-2133.2012.11004.x. [Epub ahead of print].

[4] Eaton SB, Konner M, Shostak M. Stone agers in the fast lane: chronic degenerative diseases in evolutionary perspective. Am J Med. 1988;84(4):739-749.

[5] Council on Physical Therapy. Regulation to govern advertising of ultraviolet generators to the medical profession only. JAMA. 1925;98:400.

[6] Holgate ST. The epidemic of allergy and asthma. Nature. 1999;402(6760 Suppl):B2-B4.

[7] Berin MC, Sampson HA. Food allergy: an enigmatic epidemic. Trends Immunol. 2013;34(8):390-397.

[8] Penniston KL, Tanumihardjo SA. The acute and chronic toxic effects of vitamin A. Am J Clin Nutr. 2006;83(2):191-201.

[9] Hyman SL, Stewart PA, Schmidt B, Cain U, Lemcke N, Foley JT, et al. Nutrient intake from food in children with autism. Pediatrics. 2012;130 Suppl 2:S145-S153.

[10] Cannell JJ, Vieth R, Willett W, Zasloff M, et al. Cod liver oil, vitamin A toxicity, frequent respiratory infections, and the vitamin D deficiency epidemic. Ann Otol Rhinol Laryngol. 2008;117(11):864-870.

[11] Altman DJ. The roles of the pharmaceutical industry and drug development in dermatology and dermatologic health care. Dermatol Clin. 2000;18(2):287-296.

[12] No authors listed. Harmful effects of ultraviolet radiation. Council on Scientific Affairs. JAMA. 1989;262(3):380-384.

[13] Dobbinson SJ, Wakefield MA, Jamsen KM, et al. Weekend sun protection and sunburn in Australia trends (1987-2002) and association with SunSmart television advertising. Am J Prev Med. 2008;34(2):94-101.

[14] Castleman M. Sunscam. Available at: http://www.motherjones.com/politics/1998/05/sunscam. Accessed July 26, 2014.

[15] Dixon HG, Lagerlund M, Spittal MJ, Hill DJ, Dobbinson SJ, Wakefield MA. Use of sun-protective clothing at outdoor leisure settings from 1992 to 2002: Serial cross-sectional observation survey. Cancer Epidemiol Biomarkers Prev. 2008;17(2):428-434. Epub 2008 Feb 4.

[16] Lindquist, et al. Avoidance of sun exposure is a risk factor for all-cause mortality: results from the Melanoma in Southern Sweden cohort. Intern Med 2014; 276(1): 77-86.

[17] Grant WB. In defense of the sun: An estimate of changes in mortality rates in the United States if mean serum 25-hydroxyvitamin D levels were raised to 45 ng/mL by solar ultraviolet-B irradiance. Dermatoendocrinol. 2009;1(4):207-214.

[18] Arends J. Vitamin D in oncology. Forsch Komplementmed. 2011;18(4):176-184. doi: 10.1159/000330725. Epub 2011 Aug 1. Review.

[19] Bikle DD, Elalieh H, Welsh J, Oh D, Cleaver J, Teichert A. Protective role of vitamin D signaling in skin cancer formation. J Steroid Biochem Mol Biol. 2013;136:271-279.

[20] Bikle DD. Vitamin D and the skin: Physiology and pathophysiology. Rev Endocr Metab Disord. 2012;13(1):3-19.

[21] Fleet JC, DeSmet M, Johnson R, Li Y. Vitamin D and cancer: a review of molecular mechanisms. Biochem J. 2012;441(1):61-76.

[22] Kittler H, Binder M, Wolff K, Pehamberger H. A ten-year analysis of demographic trends for cutaneous melanoma: analysis of 2,501 cases treated at the University Department of Dermatology in Vienna (1990-1999). Wien Klin Wochenschr. 2001;113(9):321-327.

[23] Rivers JK. Is there more than one road to melanoma? Lancet. 2004;363(9410):728-730.

[24] Vågero D, Ringbäck G, Kiviranta H. Melanoma and other tumors of the skin among office, other indoor and outdoor workers in Sweden 1961-1979. Br J Cancer. 1986;53(4):507-512.

[25] Lowe GC, Saavedra A, Reed KB, Velazquez AI, Dronca RS, Markovic SN, et al. Increasing incidence of melanoma among middle-aged adults: an epidemiologic study in Olmsted County, Minnesota. Mayo Clin Proc. 2014;89(1):52-59.

[26] Levell NJ, Beattie CC, Shuster S, Greenberg DC. Melanoma epidemic: a mid-summer night's dream? Br J Dermatol. 2009;161(3):630-634.

[27] Nielsen K, Måsbäck A, Olsson H, Ingvar C. A prospective, population-based study of 40,000 women regarding host factors, UV exposure and sunbed use in relation to risk and anatomic site of cutaneous melanoma. Int J Cancer. 2012;131(3):706-715.

[28] Valsesia A, Rimoldi D, Martinet D, Ibberson M, Benaglio P, Quadroni M, et al. Network-guided analysis of genes with altered somatic copy number and gene expression reveals pathways commonly perturbed in metastatic melanoma. PLoS One. 2011;6(4):e18369.

[29] Swerlick RA, Chen S. The melanoma epidemic: more apparent than real? Mayo Clin Proc. 1997;72(6):559-564.

[30] Usher-Smith JA, Emery J, Kassianos AP, Walter FM. Risk prediction models for melanoma: A systematic review. Cancer Epidemiol Biomarkers Prev. 2014;23(8):1450-1463.

[31] Osborne JE, Hutchinson PE. Vitamin D and systemic cancer: is this relevant to malignant melanoma? Br J Dermatol. 2002;147(2):197-213.

[32] Grant WB. Ecological studies of the UVB-vitamin D–cancer hypothesis. Anticancer Res. 2012;32(1):223-236.

[33] van der Rhee HJ, de Vries E, Coebergh JW. Does sunlight prevent cancer? A systematic review. Eur J Cancer. 2006;42(14):2222-2232. Epub 2006 Aug 10.

[34] Tran B, Lucas R, Kimlin M, Whiteman D, Neale R; Australian Cancer Study. Association between ambient ultraviolet radiation and risk of esophageal cancer. Am J Gastroenterol. 2012;107(12):1803-1813.

[35] Tran B, Jordan SJ, Lucas R, Webb PM, Neale R; Australian Ovarian Cancer Study Group. Association between ambient ultraviolet radiation and risk of epithelial ovarian cancer. Cancer Prev Res (Phila). 2012;5(11):1330-1336.

[36] Boscoe FP, Schymura MJ. Solar ultraviolet-B exposure and cancer incidence and mortality in the United States, 1993-2002. BMC Cancer. 2006;6:264.

[37] D'Orazio J, Jarrett S, Amaro-Ortiz A, Scott T. UV radiation and the skin. Int J Mol Sci. 2013;14(6):12222-12248.

[38] Kaur M, Liguori A, Lang W, Rapp SR, Fleischer AB Jr, Feldman SR. Induction of withdrawal-like symptoms in a small randomized, controlled trial of opioid blockade in frequent tanners. J Am Acad Dermatol. 2006;54(4):709-711.

[39] Cantorna MT, Hayes CE, DeLuca HF. 1,25-Dihydroxyvitamin D_3 reversibly blocks the progression of relapsing encephalomyelitis, a model of multiple sclerosis. Proc Natl Acad Sci U S A. 1996;93(15):7861-7864.

[40] 40 Wang Y, Marling SJ, McKnight SM, Danielson AL, Severson KS, Deluca HF.

Suppression of experimental autoimmune encephalomyelitis by 300-315nm ultraviolet light. Arch Biochem Biophys. 2013 Aug 1;536(1):81-6.

[41] Lucas RM, Ponsonby AL, Dear K, Valery PC, Pender MP, Taylor BV, et al. Sun exposure and vitamin D are independent risk factors for CNS demyelination. Neurology. 2011;76(6):540-548.

Chapter Five

[1] Hiraki LT, Major JM, Chen C, Cornelis MC, Hunter DJ, Rim EB, et al. Exploring the genetic architecture of circulating 25-hydroxyvitamin D. Genet Epidemiology. 2013;37(1):92-98. doi: 10.1002/gepi.21694. Pub 2012 Nov 7.

[2] An J, Yu K, Stoltenberg-Solomon R, Simon KC, McCullough ML, Galicia L, et al. Genome-wide association study of circulating vitamin D levels. Hum Mol Genet. 2010;19(13):2739-2745.

[3] Wang TJ, Zhang F, Richards JB, Kirshenbaum B, van Moors JB, Berry D, et al. Common genetic determinants of vitamin D insufficiency: a genome-wide association study. Lancet. 2010;376(9736):180-188.

[4] Arguelles LM, Langman CB, Ariza AJ, Ali FN, Dilley K, Price H, et al. Heritability and environmental factors affecting vitamin D status in rural Chinese adolescent twins. J Clin Endocrinol Metab. 2009;94(9):3273-3281.

[5] Schnatz PF, Nudy M, O'Sullivan DM, Jiang X, Cline JM, Kaplan JR, et al. The quantification of vitamin D receptors in coronary arteries and their association with atherosclerosis. Maturitas. 2012;73:143-147. doi: 10.1016/j.maturitas.2012.03.014.

[6] Epstein S, Schneider AE. Drug and hormone effects on vitamin D metabolism. In: Feldman D, Pike JW, Glorieux FH, eds. Vitamin D. San Diego: Elsevier; 2005.

[7] Cannell JJ, Hollis BW, Castoff M, Heaney RP. Diagnosis and treatment of vitamin D deficiency. Expert Open Pharmacotherapy. 2008;9(1):107-118.

[8] Holick M. Does sunscreen block the skin's ability to make vitamin D? If so, how can I get enough of this vitamin without raising my risk of skin cancer? Health News. 2002;8(7):12.

[9] Hossein-Nezhad A, Holick MF. Vitamin D for health: A global perspective. Mayo Clin Proc. 2013;88(7):720-755.

[10] Thomas MK, Lloyd-Jones DM, Thadhani RI, et al. Hypovitaminosis D in medical inpatients. N Engl J Med. 1998;338(12):777-783.

[11] Luxwolda MF, Kuipers RS, Kema IP, van der Veer E, Dijck-Brouwer DA, Muskiet FA. Vitamin D status indicators in indigenous populations in East Africa. Eur J Nutr. 2013;52(3):1115-1125.

[12] Luxwolda MF, Kuipers RS, Kema IP, Dijck-Brouwer DA, Muskiet FA. Traditionally living populations in East Africa have a mean serum 25-hydroxyvitamin D concentration of 115 nmol/l. Br J Nutr. 2012;108(9):1157-1161. [Epub ahead of print]

[13] Premaor MO, Paludo P, Manica D, Paludo AP, Rossatto ER, Scalco R, et al. Hypovitaminosis D and secondary hyperparathyroidism in resident physicians of a general hospital in southern Brazil. J Endocrinol Invest. 2008;31(11):991-995.

[14] Dawodu A, Wagner CL. Prevention of vitamin D deficiency in mothers and infants worldwide - a paradigm shift. Paediatr Int Child Health. 2012;32(1):3-13.

[15] Holick MF, Binkley NC, Bischoff-Ferrari HA, Gordon CM, Hanley DA, Heaney RP, et al; Endocrine Society. Evaluation, treatment, and prevention of vitamin D deficiency: an Endocrine Society clinical practice guideline. J Clin Endocrinol Metab. 2011;96(7):1911-1930.

[16] Spedding S, Vanlint S, Morris H, Scragg R. Does vitamin D sufficiency equate to a single serum 25-hydroxyvitamin D level or are different levels required for non-skeletal diseases? Nutrients. 2013;5(12):5127-5139.

[17] Hollis BW, Wagner CL. The vitamin D requirement during human lactation: the facts and IOM's "utter" failure. Public Health Nutr. 2011;14(4):748-749.

[18] Haggerty LL. Maternal supplementation for prevention and treatment of vitamin D deficiency in exclusively breastfed infants. Breastfeed Med. 2011;6(3):137-144. Epub 2010 Oct 29.

[19] Ginde AA, Liu MC, Camargo CA Jr. Demographic differences and trends of vitamin D insufficiency in the US population, 1988-2004. Arch Intern Med. 2009;169(6):626-632.

[20] Cannell JJ. Vitamin D and autism. Med Hypotheses. 2008;70(4):750-759.

[21] Grant WB, Cannell JJ. Autism prevalence in the United States with respect to solar UV-B doses: An ecological study. Dermatoendocrinol. 2013;5(1):159-164.

[22] Hanieh S, Ha TT, Simpson JA, Thuy TT, Khuong NC, Thoang DD, et al. Maternal vitamin D status and infant outcomes in rural Vietnam: A prospective cohort study. PLOS One. 201426(9):e99005.

[23] Kočovská E, Fernell E, Billstedt E, Minnis H, Gillberg C. Vitamin D and autism: Clinical review. Res Dev Disabil. 2012;33(5):1541-1550. [Epub ahead of print]

[24] Bell DS. Protean manifestations of vitamin D deficiency, part 2: deficiency and its association with autoimmune disease, cancer, infection, asthma, dermopathies, insulin resistance, and type 2 diabetes. South Med J. 2011;104(5):335-339.

[25] Bell DS. Protean manifestations of vitamin D deficiency, part 3: association with cardiovascular disease and disorders of the central and peripheral nervous systems. South Med J. 2011;104(5):340-344.

[26] Cannell JJ, Zasloff M, Garland CF, Scragg R, Giovannucci E. On the epidemiology of influenza. Virol J. 2008;5:29.

[27] Cannell JJ, Vieth R, Umhau JC, Holick MF, Grant WB, Madronich S, et al. Epidemic influenza and vitamin D. Epidemiol Infect. 2006;134(6):1129-1140.

[28] Urashima M, Segawa T, Okazaki M, Kurihara M, Wada Y, Ida H. Randomized trial of vitamin D supplementation to prevent seasonal influenza A in school-children. Am J Clin Nutr. 2010;91(5):1255-1260.

[29] White JH. Vitamin D as an inducer of cathelicidin antimicrobial peptide expression: past, present and future. J Steroid Biochem Mol Biol. 2010;121(1-2):234-238. Epub 2010 Mar 17.

[30] Thompson WW, Shay DK, Weintraub E, Brammer L, Bridges CB, Cox NJ, et al. Influenza-associated hospitalizations in the United States. JAMA. 2004;292:1333-1340.

[31] Thompson WW, Shay DK, Weintraub E, Brammer L, Cox N, Anderson LJ, et al. Mortality associated with influenza and respiratory syncytial virus in the United States. JAMA. 2003;289:179-186.

[32] Aloia JF, Li-Ng M. Re: epidemic influenza and vitamin D. Epidemiol Infect. 2007;135(7):1095-1096; author reply 1097-1098. No abstract available.

[33] Bergman P, Lindh AU, Björkhem-Bergman L, Lindh JD. Vitamin D and respiratory tract infections: A systematic review and meta-analysis of randomized controlled trials. PLoS One. 2013;8(6):e65835.

[34] Murdoch DR, Slow S, Chambers ST, Jennings LC, Stewart AW, Priest PC, et al. Effect of vitamin D_3 supplementation on upper respiratory tract infections in healthy adults: the VIDARIS randomized controlled trial. JAMA. 2012;308(13):1333-1339.

[35] University of California at San Francisco. Open-label clinical trial of vitamin D in children with autism. Available at: https://clinicaltrials.gov/ct2/show/NCT01535 508?term=vitamin+D+and+autism&rank=2. Accessed July 1, 2014.

[36] Saad K, Cannell JJ, Bjorklund G, Abdel-Reheim MK. Vitamin D status in autism spectrum disorder and the efficacy of vitamin D supplementation in autistic children. Submitted for publication.

Chapter Six

[1] Developmental Disabilities Monitoring Network Surveillance Year 2010 Principal Investigators; Centers for Disease Control and Prevention (CDC). Prevalence of autism spectrum disorder among children aged 8 years - Autism and Developmental Disabilities Monitoring Network, 11 sites, United States, 2010. MMWR Surveill Summ. 2014;63(2):1-21.

[2] Bhasin TK, Schendel D. Sociodemographic risk factors for autism in a US metropolitan area. J Autism Dev Disord 2007;37(4):667-677.

[3] Croen LA, Grether JK, Hoogstrate J, Selvin S. The changing prevalence of autism in California. J Autism Dev Disord 2002;32(3):207-215.

[4] Hillman RE, Kanafani N, Takahashi TN, Miles JH. Prevalence of autism in Missouri: changing trends and the effect of a comprehensive state autism project. Mo Med 2000;97(5):159-163.

[5] Yeargin-Allsopp M, Rice C, Karapurkar T, Doernberg N, Boyle C, Murphy C. Prevalence of autism in a US metropolitan area. JAMA 2003;289(1):49-55.

[6] Becerra TA, von Ehrenstein OS, Heck JE, Olsen J, Arah OA, Jeste SS, et al. Autism spectrum disorders and race, ethnicity, and nativity: a population-based study. Pediatrics. 2014;134(1):e63-71.

[7] Patrick RP, Ames BN. Vitamin D hormone regulates serotonin synthesis. Part 1: relevance for autism. FASEB J. 2014;28(6):2398-2413. Epub 2014 Feb 20.

[8] Goodman R, Richards H. Child and adolescent psychiatric presentations of second-generation Afro-Caribbeans in Britain. Br J Psychiatry 1995;167(3):362-369.

[9] Keen DV, Reid FD, Amone D. Autism, ethnicity and maternal immigration. Br J Psychiatry. 2010 April;196(4):274-281.

[10] Dealberto MJ. Prevalence of autism according to maternal immigrant status and ethnic origin. Acta Psychiatr Scand. 2011;123(5):339-348. doi: 10.1111/j.1600-0447.2010.01662.x. Epub 2011 Jan 11.

[11] Barnevik-Olsson M, Gillberg C, Fernell E. Prevalence of autism in children born to Somali parents living in Sweden: A brief report. Dev Med Child Neuro. 2008;50(8):598-601.

[12] Gillberg IC, Gillberg C. Autism in immigrants: A population-based study in Swedish rural and urban areas. J Intellect Disabil Res. 1996;40 (Pt 1):24-31.

[13] Gillberg C, Schaumann H, Gillberg IC. Autism in immigrants: Children born in Sweden to mothers born in Uganda. J Intellect Disabil Res. 1995;39 (Pt. 2):141-144.

[14] Gorman E. A mysterious connection: autism and Minneapolis' Somali children. StarTribune. July 24, 2008.

[15] Kirby D. Is autism an "American disease?" Somali immigrants reportedly have high rates. Huffington Post. July 7, 2008.

[16] Yeargin-Allsopp M, Drews CD, Decoufle P, Murphy CC. Mild mental retardation in black and white children in metropolitan Atlanta: a case-control study. Am J Public Health. 1995;85(3):324-328.

[17] Cabacungan ET, Ngui EM, McGinley EL. Racial/ethnic disparities in maternal morbidities: A statewide study of labor and delivery hospitalizations in Wisconsin. Matern Child Health J 2011 Nov 22.

[18] Guinchat V, Thorsen P, Laurent C, Cans C, Bodeau N, Cohen D. Pre-, peri- and neonatal risk factors for autism. Acta Obstet Gynecol Scand. 2012;91(3):287-300.

[19] Cabacungan ET, Ngui EM, McGinley EL. Racial/ethnic disparities in maternal

morbidities: A statewide study of labor and delivery hospitalizations in Wisconsin. Matern Child Health J. 2012;16(7):1455-1467.

20 Larsson HJ, Eaton WW, Madsen KM, Vestergaard M, Olesen AV, Agerbo E, et al. Risk factors for autism: perinatal factors, parental psychiatric history, and socioeconomic status. Am J Epidemiol. 2005;161(10):916-925; discussion 926-928.

21 Hultman CM, Sparén P, Cnattingius S. Perinatal risk factors for infantile autism. Epidemiology. 2002;13(4):417-423.

22 Dixon B, Peña MM, Taveras EM. Lifecourse approach to racial/ethnic disparities in childhood obesity. Adv Nutr. 2012;3(1):73-82. Epub 2012 Jan 5.

23 Krakowiak P, Walker CK, Bremer AA, Baker AS, Ozonoff S, Hansen RL, et al. Maternal metabolic conditions and risk for autism and other neurodevelopmental disorders. Pediatrics. 2012;129(5):e1121-8. Epub 2012 April 9.

24 Buescher PA, Mittal M. Racial disparities in birth outcomes increase with maternal age: recent data from North Carolina. N C Med J. 2006;67(1):16-20.

25 Nesby-O'Dell S, Scanlan KS, Cogswell ME, Gillespie C, Hollis BW, Looker AC, et al. Hypovitaminosis D prevalence and determinants among African American and white women of reproductive age: third National Health and Nutrition Examination Survey, 1988-1994. Am J Clin Nutr. 2002;76(1):187-192.

26 Bodnar LM, Simhan HN, Powers RW, Frank MP, Cooperstein E, Roberts JM. High prevalence of vitamin D insufficiency in black and white pregnant women residing in the northern United States and their neonates. J Nutr. 2007;137(2):447-452.

27 Luxwolda MF, Kuipers RS, Kema IP, Dijck-Brouwer DA, Muskiet FA. Traditionally living populations in East Africa have a mean serum 25-hydroxyvitamin D concentration of 115 nmol/l. Br J Nutr. 2012;108(9):1557-1561.

28 Grant WB, Peiris AN. Possible role of serum 25-hydroxyvitamin D in black–white health disparities in the United States. J Am Med Directors Assoc. 2010;11(9):617-628.

29 Grant WB, Peiris AN. Differences in vitamin D status may account for unexplained disparities in cancer survival rates between African and white Americans. Dermatoendocrinol. 2012;4(2):85-94.

30 Jemal A, Murray T, Ward E, Samuels A, Tiwari RC, Ghafoor A, et al. Cancer statistics, 2005. CA Cancer J Clin. 2005;55(1):10-30.

31 Chronic Disease Epidemiology and Control, Second Edition. American Public Health Association, 1998.

32 Schwartz GG, Skinner HG. Vitamin D status and cancer: new insights. Curr Opin Clin Nutr Metab Care. 2007;10(1):6-11.

[33] Vuolo L, Di Somma C, Faggiano A, Colao A. Vitamin D and cancer. Front Endocrinol (Lausanne). 2012;3:58. Epub 2012 Apr 23.

[34] Clark LT. Issues in minority health: atherosclerosis and coronary heart disease in African Americans. Med Clin North Am. 2005;89(5):977-1001, 994.

[35] Kendrick J, Targher G, Smits G, Chonchol M. 25-Hydroxyvitamin D deficiency is independently associated with cardiovascular disease in the Third National Health and Nutrition Examination Survey. Atherosclerosis. 2009;205(1):255-260. Epub 2008 Nov 11.

[36] Kleindorfer D, Broderick J, Khoury J, Flaherty M, Woo D, Alwell K, et al. The unchanging incidence and case-fatality of stroke in the 1990s: a population-based study. Stroke. 2006;37(10):2473-2478. Epub 2006 Aug 31.

[37] Poole KE, Loveridge N, Barker PJ, Halsall DJ, Rose C, Reeve J, et al. Reduced vitamin D in acute stroke. Stroke. 2006;37(1):243-245. Epub 2005 December 1.

[38] Lopes AA, James SA, Port FK, Ojo AO, Agodoa LY, Jamerson KA. Meeting the challenge to improve the treatment of hypertension in blacks. J Clin Hypertens (Greenwich). 2003;5(6):393-401.

[39] Forman JP, Curhan GC, Taylor EN. Plasma 25-hydroxyvitamin D levels and risk of incident hypertension among young women. Hypertension. 2008;52(5):828-832.

[40] Egede LE, Dagogo-Jack S. Epidemiology of type 2 diabetes: focus on ethnic minorities. Med Clin North Am. 2005;89(5):949-975, viii.

[41] Hyppönen E, Power C. Vitamin D status and glucose homeostasis in the 1958 British birth cohort: the role of obesity. Diabetes Care. 2006;29(10):2244-2246.

[42] Price DA, Crook ED. Kidney disease in African Americans: genetic considerations. J Natl Med Assoc. 2002;94(8 Suppl):16S-27S.

[43] Gonzàlez EA, Sachdeva A, Oliver DA, Martin KJ. Vitamin D insufficiency and deficiency in chronic kidney disease. A single center observational study. Am J Nephrol. 2004;24(5):503-510. Epub 2004 Sept 22.

[44] LaClair RE, Hellman RN, Karp SL, Kraus M, Ofner S, Li Q, et al. Prevalence of calcidiol deficiency in CKD: a cross-sectional study across latitudes in the United States. Am J Kidney Dis. 2005;45(6):1026-1033.

[45] Weinstock-Guttman B, Jacobs LD, Brownscheidle CM, Baier M, Rea DF, Apatoff BR. Multiple sclerosis characteristics in African American patients in the New York State Multiple Sclerosis Consortium. Mult Scler. 2003;9(3):293-298.

[46] Munger KL, Levin LI, Hollis BW, Howard NS, Ascherio A. Serum 25-hydroxyvitamin D levels and risk of multiple sclerosis. JAMA. 2006;296(23):2832-2838.

[47] Sacks JJ, Helmick CG, Langmaid G. Deaths from arthritis and other rheumatic conditions, United States, 1979-1998. J Rheumatol. 2004;31(9):1823-1828.

[48] Abourazzak FE, Talbi S, Aradoini N, Berrada K, Keita S, Hazry T. 25-hydroxy vitamin D and its relationship with clinical and laboratory parameters in patients with rheumatoid arthritis. Clin Rheumatol. 2014 Jun 13. [Epub ahead of print]

[49] Cannell JJ, Vieth R, Umhau JC, Holick MF, Grant WB, Madronich S, et al. Epidemic influenza and vitamin D. Epidemiol Infect. 2006;134(6):1129-40. Epub 2006 Sept 7.

[50] Bergman P, Lindh AU, Björkhem-Bergman L, Lindh JD. Vitamin D and respiratory tract infections: A systematic review and meta-analysis of randomized controlled trials. PLoS One. 2013;8(6):e65835.

[51] Craig RG, Yip JK, Mijares DQ, Boylan RJ, Haffajee AD, Socransky SS. Destructive periodontal diseases in minority populations. Dent Clin North Am. 2003;47(1):103-114, x.

[52] Dietrich T, Joshipura KJ, Dawson-Hughes B, Bischoff-Ferrari HA. Association between serum concentrations of 25-hydroxyvitamin D_3 and periodontal disease in the US population. Am J Clin Nutr. 2004;80(1):108-113.

Chapter Seven

[1] Cannell JJ, Hollis BW, Zasloff M, Heaney RP. Diagnosis and treatment of vitamin D deficiency. Expert Opin Pharmacother. 2008;9(1):107-118.

[2] Adams JS, Clemens TL, Parrish JA, Holick MF. Vitamin D synthesis and metabolism after ultraviolet irradiation of normal and vitamin-D-deficient subjects. N Engl J Med. 1982;306(12):722-725.

[3] Dart RC, Paul IM, Bond GR, Winston DC, Manoguerra AS, Palmer RB, et al. Pediatric fatalities associated with over the counter (nonprescription) cough and cold medications. Ann Emerg Med. 2009;53(4):411-417.

[4] Vieth R. Critique of the considerations for establishing the tolerable upper intake level for vitamin D: critical need for revision upwards. J Nutr. 2006;136(4):1117-1122.

[5] Cannell JJ, Hollis BW. Use of vitamin D in clinical practice. Altern Med Rev. 2008;13(1):6-20.

[6] Sundar IK, Rahman I. Vitamin D and susceptibility of chronic lung diseases: Role of epigenetics. Front Pharmacol. 2011;2:50. Epub 2011 Aug 30.

[7] Cannell J. Era or error? Public Health Nutr. 2011;14(4):743.

[8] Haussler MR, Jurutka PW, Mizwicki M, Norman AW. Vitamin D receptor (VDR)-mediated actions of $1\alpha,25(OH)_2$vitamin D_3: Genomic and non-genomic mechanisms. Best Pract Res Clin Endocrinol Metab. 2011;25(4):543-559.

[9] Heaney RP. Assessing vitamin D status. Curr Opin Clin Nutr Metab Care. 2011;14(5):440-444.

[10] Tavera-Mendoza LE, White JH. Cell defenses and the sunshine vitamin. Sci Am. 2007;297(5):62-65, 68-70, 72.

[11] Walker RB, Conn JA, Davies MJ, Moore VM. Mothers' views on feeding infants around the time of weaning. Public Health Nutr. 2006;9(6):707-713.

[12] Perrine CG, Sharma AJ, Jefferds ME, Serdula MK, Scanlon KS. Adherence to vitamin D recommendations among US infants. Pediatrics. 2010;125(4):627-632.

[13] Hall HI, Jorgensen CM, McDavid K, Kraft JM, Breslow R. Protection from sun exposure in US white children ages 6 months to 11 years. Public Health Rep. 2001;116(4):353-361.

[14] Stumpf WE. Vitamin D—soltriol, the heliogenic steroid hormone: Somatotrophic activator and modulator. Discoveries from histochemical studies lead to new concepts. Histochemistry. 1988;89(3):209-219.

Chapter Eight

[1] Timmer J. Schizophrenia: Genes matter (even though inheritance might not). Available at: http://arstechnica.com/science/2011/08/genetics-is-key-schizophrenia-even-when-inheritance-isnt/. Accessed June 4, 2014.

[2] Sanders SJ, Murtha MT, Gupta AR, Murdoch JD, Raubeson MJ, Willsey AJ, et al. De novo mutations revealed by whole-exome sequencing are strongly associated with autism. Nature. 2012;485(7397):237-241. doi: 10.1038/nature10945. [Epub ahead of print]

[3] Fleet JC, DeSmet M, Johnson R, Li Y. Vitamin D and cancer: A review of molecular mechanisms. Biochem J. 2012;441(1):61-76.

[4] Halicka HD, Zhao H, Li J, Traganos F, Studzinski GP, Darzynkiewicz Z. Attenuation of constitutive DNA damage signaling by 1,25-dihydroxyvitamin D_3. Aging (Albany, NY). 2012;4(4):270-278.

[5] Ting HJ, Yasmin-Karim S, Yan SJ, Hsu JW, Lin TH, Zeng W, et al. A positive feedback signaling loop between ATM and the vitamin D receptor is critical for cancer chemoprevention by vitamin D. Cancer Res. 2012;72(4):958-968. Epub 2011 Dec 29.

[6] Chatterjee M. Vitamin D and genomic stability. Mutat Res. 2001;475(1-2):69-87.

[7] Nair-Shalliker V, Armstrong BK, Fenech M. Does vitamin D protect against DNA damage? Mutat Res. 2012;733(1-2):50-57.

[8] Malik M, Sheikh AM, Wen G, Spivack W, Brown WT, Li X. Expression of inflammatory cytokines, Bcl2 and cathepsin D are altered in lymphoblasts of autistic subjects. Immunobiology. 2011;216(1-2):80-85. Epub 2010 Mar 12.

[9] Guillot X, Semerano L, Saidenberg-Kermanac'h N, Falgarone G, Boissier MC. Vitamin D and inflammation. Joint Bone Spine. 2010;77(6):552-557. Epub 2010 Nov 9.

[10] Bischoff-Ferrari HA, Dawson-Hughes B, Stöcklin E, Sidelnikov E, Willett WC, et al. Oral supplementation with 25(OH)D$_3$ versus vitamin D$_3$: effects on 25(OH)D levels, lower extremity function, blood pressure, and markers of innate immunity. J Bone Miner Res. 2012;27(1):160-169.

[11] Bucharles S, Barberato SH, Stinghen AE, Gruber B, Piekala L, Dambiski AC, et al. Impact of cholecalciferol treatment on biomarkers of inflammation and myocardial structure in hemodialysis patients without hyperparathyroidism. J Ren Nutr. 2012;22(2):284-291.

[12] Mahon BD, Gordon SA, Cruz J, Cosman F, Cantorna MT. Cytokine profile in patients with multiple sclerosis following vitamin D supplementation. J Neuroimmunol. 2003;134(1-2):128-132.

[13] Abou-Raya A, Abou-Raya S, Helmii M. The effect of vitamin D supplementation on inflammatory and hemostatic markers and disease activity in patients with systemic lupus erythematosus: a randomized placebo-controlled trial. J Rheumatol. 2013;40(3):265-272.

[14] Coussens AK, Wilkinson RJ, Hanifa Y, Nikolayevskyy V, Elkington PT, Islam K, et al. Vitamin D accelerates resolution of inflammatory responses during tuberculosis treatment. Proc Natl Acad Sci U S A. 2012;109(38):15449-15454. Epub 2012 Sept 4.

[15] Gao D, Trayhurn P, Bing C. 1,25-Dihydroxyvitamin D(3) inhibits the cytokine-induced secretion of MCP-1 and reduces monocyte recruitment by human preadipocytes. Int J Obes (Lond). 2013;37(3):357-365. doi: 10.1038/ijo.2012.53. [Epub ahead of print]

[16] Shedeed SA. Vitamin D supplementation in infants with chronic congestive heart failure. Pediatr Cardiol. 2012;33(5):713-719. [Epub ahead of print]

[17] Krishnan AV, Feldman D. Molecular pathways mediating the anti-inflammatory effects of calcitriol: implications for prostate cancer chemoprevention and treatment. Endocr Relat Cancer. 2010;17(1):R19-R38.

[18] Qin W, Smith C, Jensen M, Holick MF, Sauter ER. Vitamin D favorably alters the cancer promoting prostaglandin cascade. Anticancer Res. 2013;33(9):3861-3866.

[19] Ziats MN, Rennert OM. Expression profiling of autism candidate genes during human brain development implicates central immune signaling pathways. PLoS One. 2011;6(9):e24691. Epub 2011 Sep 15.

[20] Delvin E, Souberbielle JC, Viard JP, Salle B. Role of vitamin D in acquired immune and autoimmune diseases. Crit Rev Clin Lab Sci. 2014;51(4):232-247.

[21] Lemire JM. Immunomodulatory role of 1,25-dihydroxyvitamin D$_3$. J Cell Biochem. 1992;49(1):26-31.

[22] Muñoz LE, Schiller M, Zhao Y, Voll RE, Schett G, Herrmann M. Do low vitamin D levels cause problems of waste removal in patients with SLE? Rheumatology (Oxford). 2012;51(4):585-587. Epub 2011 Oct 27.

[23] Hayes CE, Nashold FE, Spach KM, Pedersen LB. The immunological functions of the vitamin D endocrine system. Cell Mol Biol (Noisy-le-grand). 2003;49(2):277-300.

[24] Al-Ayadhi LY. Reduced serum concentrations of 25-hydroxy vitamin D in children with autism: relation to autoimmunity. J Neuroinflammation. 2012;9:201.

[25] Hara H. Autism and epilepsy: a retrospective follow-up study. Brain Dev. 2007.29(8):486-490. Epub 2007 Feb 26.

[26] Holló A, Clemens Z, Kamondi A, Lakatos P, Szűcs A. Correction of vitamin D deficiency improves seizure control in epilepsy: A pilot study. Epilepsy Behav. 2012;24(1):131-133.

[27] Prietl B, Pilz S, Wolf M, Tomaschitz A, Obermayer-Pietsch B, Graninger W, et al. Vitamin D supplementation and regulatory T cells in apparently healthy subjects: vitamin D treatment for autoimmune diseases? Isr Med Assoc J. 2010;12(3):136-139.

[28] Pedersen AW, Claesson MH, Zocca MB. Dendritic cells modified by vitamin D: future immunotherapy for autoimmune diseases. Vitam Horm. 2011;86:63-82.

[29] Neveu I, Naveilhan P, Jehan F, Baudet C, Wion D, De Luca HF, et al. 1,25-dihydroxyvitamin D_3 regulates the synthesis of nerve growth factor in primary cultures of glial cells. Brain Res Mol Brain Res. 1994;24(1-4):70-76.

[30] Féron F, Burne TH, Brown J, Smith E, McGrath JJ, Mackay-Sim A, et al. Developmental vitamin D_3 deficiency alters the adult rat brain. Brain Res Bull. 2005;65(2):141-148.

[31] Frye RE, Rossignol DA. Mitochondrial dysfunction can connect the diverse medical symptoms associated with autism spectrum disorders. Pediatr Res. 2011;69(5 Pt 2):41R-47R.

[32] García IM, Altamirano L, Mazzei LJ, Fornés M, Molina MN, Ferder L, et al. Role of mitochondria in paracalcitol-mediated cytoprotection during obstructive nephropathy. Am J Physiol Renal Physiol. 2012;302(12):F1595-1605.

[33] Garcion E, Thanh XD, Bled F, Teissier E, Dehouck MP, Rigault F, et al. 1,25-Dihydroxy vitamin D_3 regulates gamma-glutamyl transpeptidase activity in rat brain. Neurosci Lett. 1996;216(3):183-186.

[34] Garcion E, Wion-Barbot N, Montero-Menei CN, Berger F, Wion D. New clues about vitamin D functions in the nervous system. Trends Endocrinol Metab 2002;13(3):100-105.

[35] Baas D, Prüfer K, Ittel ME, Kuchler-Bopp S, Labourdette G, Sarliève LL, et al. Rat oligodendrocytes express the vitamin D(3) receptor and respond to 1,25-dihydroxyvitamin D(3). Glia. 2000;31(1):59-68.

[36] Kern JK, Jones AM. Evidence of toxicity, oxidative stress, and neuronal insult in autism. J Toxicol Environ Health B Crit Rev. 2006;9(6):485-499.

[37] Alvarez JA, Chowdhury R, Jones DP, Martin GS, Brigham KL, Binongo JN, et al. Vitamin D status is independently associated with plasma glutathione and cysteine thiol/disulphide redox status in adults. Clin Endocrinol (Oxf). 2014 Mar 13.

[38] Buell JS, Dawson-Hughes B. Vitamin D and neurocognitive dysfunction: preventing "D"ecline? Mol Aspects Med. 2008;29(6):415-422.

[39] Lindh JD, Björkhem-Bergman L, Eliasson E. Vitamin D and drug-metabolising enzymes. Photochem Photobiol Sci. 2012;11(12):1797-1801.

Chapter Nine

[1] Institute of Medicine. Report at a glance: DRIs for Calcium and Vitamin D. 2010. Available at: http://www.iom.edu/Reports/2010/Dietary-Reference-Intakes-for-Calcium-and-Vitamin-D/DRI-Values.aspx. Accessed June 15, 2014.

[2] Food and Nutrition Board of the Institute of Medicine. Dietary Reference Intakes (DRIs): Tolerable Upper Intake Levels, Vitamins. 2010. Available at: http://iom.edu/Activities/Nutrition/SummaryDRIs/~/media/Files/Activity%20Files/Nutrition/DRIs/ULs%20for%20Vitamins%20and%20Elements.pdf. Accessed June 15, 2014.

[3] Trivedi DP, Doll R, Khaw KT. Effect of four monthly oral vitamin D_3 (cholecalciferol) supplementation on fractures and mortality in men and women living in the community: randomised double blind controlled trial. BMJ. 2003;326(7387):469.

[4] Paracelcus. Wikipedia. Available at: http://en.wikipedia.org/wiki/Paracelsus. Accessed June 26, 2014.

[5] Daud KM, Julies P, Poblete X, Jacobs B. Safety of vitamin D supplementation in children: a massive vitamin D overdose with no apparent hypercalcaemia. Arch Dis Child. 2012;97:A12 doi:10.1136/archdischild-2012-301885.28.

[6] Hyppönen E, Läärä E, Reunanen A, Järvelin MR, Virtanen SM. Intake of vitamin D and risk of type 1 diabetes: a birth-cohort study. Lancet. 2001;358(9292):1500-1503.

[7] McGrath J, Saari K, Hakko H, Jokelainen J, Jones P, Järvelin MR, et al. Vitamin D supplementation during the first year of life and risk of schizophrenia: a Finnish birth cohort study. Schizophr Res. 2004;67(2-3):237-245.

[8] Zeghoud F, Ben-Mekhbi H, Djeghri N, Garabédian M. Vitamin D prophylaxis during infancy: comparison of the long-term effects of three intermittent doses (15, 5, or 2.5 mg) on 25-hydroxyvitamin D concentrations. Am J Clin Nutr. 1994;60(3):393-396.

[9] Kunz C, von Lilienfeld-Toal H, Niesen M, Burmeister W. 25-hydroxy-vitamin-D in serum of newborns and infants during continuous oral vitamin D treatment [author's translation]. Padiatr Padol. 1982;17(2):181-185. German.

[10] Markestad T, Hesse V, Siebenhuner M, Jahreis G, Aksnes L, Plenert W, et al. Intermittent high-dose vitamin D prophylaxis during infancy: effect on vitamin D metabolites, calcium and phosphorus. Am J Clin Nutr. 1987;46(4):652-658.

[11] Hollis BW, Wagner CL. Vitamin D deficiency during pregnancy: an ongoing epidemic. Am J Clin Nutr. 2006;84(2):273.

[12] Vitamin D Supplementation: Recommendations for Canadian Mothers and Infants. Canadian Paediatric Society. Available at: http://www.cps.ca/documents/position/vitamin-d. Accessed June 26, 2014.

[13] Hollis BW, Wagner CL. Vitamin D and pregnancy: Skeletal effects, nonskeletal effects, and birth outcomes. Calcif Tissue Int. 2013;92(2):128-139. Epub 2012 May 24.

[14] Vieth R. Vitamin D supplementation, 25-hydroxyvitamin D concentrations, and safety. Am J Clin Nutr. 1999;69(5):842-856.

[15] Barrueto F Jr, Wang-Flores HH, Howland MA, Hoffman RS, Nelson LS. Acute vitamin D intoxication in a child. Pediatrics. 2005;116(3):e453-e456.

[16] Overholt EL. Water intoxication: its diagnosis and management. Mil Med. 1968;133(8):607-613.

[17] Heaney RP, Davies KM, Chen TC, Holick MF, Barger-Lux MJ. Human serum 25-hydroxycholecalciferol response to extended oral dosing with cholecalciferol. Am J Clin Nutr. 2003;77(1):204-210.

[18] Adams JS, Clemens TL, Parrish JA, Holick MF. Vitamin-D synthesis and metabolism after ultraviolet irradiation of normal and vitamin-D–deficient subjects. N Engl J Med. 1982;306(12):722-725.

[19] Holick MF. Vitamin D: a d-lightful solution for health. J Investig Med. 2011;59(6):872-880.

[20] Holick MF. Environmental factors that influence the cutaneous production of vitamin D. Am J Clin Nutr. 1995;61(3 Suppl):638S-645S.

[21] Heaney RP. Vitamin D in health and disease. Clin J Am Soc Nephrol. 2008;3(5):1535-1541. Epub 2008 Jun 4.

[22] Bronstein AC, Spyker DA, Cantilena LR Jr, Green JL, Rumack BH, Dart RC. 2010 Annual Report of the American Association of Poison Control Centers' National Poison Data System (NPDS): 28th Annual Report. Clin Toxicol (Phila). 2011;49(10):910-941.

[23] Koutkia P, Chen TC, Holick MF. Vitamin D intoxication associated with an over-the-counter supplement. N Engl J Med. 2001;345(1):66-67.

[24] Vieth R, Pinto TR, Reen BS, Wong MM. Vitamin D poisoning by table sugar. Lancet. 2002;359(9307):672.

Chapter Ten
[1] Vanstone MB, Oberfield SE, Shader L, Ardeshirpour L, Carpenter TO. Hyper-

calcemia in children receiving pharmacologic doses of vitamin D. Pediatrics. 2012;129(4):e1060-1063.

[2] Penniston KL, Tanumihardjo SA. The acute and chronic toxic effects of vitamin A. Am J Clin Nutr. 2006;83(2):191-201.

[3] Cannell JJ, Vieth R, Willett W, Zasloff M, Hathcock JN, White JH, et al. Cod liver oil, vitamin A toxicity, frequent respiratory infections, and the vitamin D deficiency epidemic. Ann Otol Rhinol Laryngol. 2008;117(11):864-870.

[4] Galland L. Magnesium, stress and neuropsychiatric disorders. Magnes Trace Elem. 1991-1992;10(2-4):287-301.

[5] Zofková I, Kancheva RL. The relationship between magnesium and calciotropic hormones. Magnes Res. 1995;8(1):77–84.

[6] Ford ES, Mokdad AH. Dietary magnesium intake in a national sample of US adults. J Nutr. 2003;133(9):2879–2882.

[7] Davison KM, Kaplan BJ. Nutrient intakes are correlated with overall psychiatric functioning in adults with mood disorders. Can J Psychiatry. 2012;57(2):85-92.

[8] Jacka FN, Maes M, Pasco JA, Williams LJ, Berk M. Nutrient intakes and the common mental disorders in women. J Affect Disord. 2012 Mar 5.

[9] Yasuda H, Yoshida K, Yasuda Y, Tsutsui T. Infantile zinc deficiency: association with autism spectrum disorders. Sci Rep. 2011;1:129.

[10] Fujii S, Masuno H, Taoda Y, Kano A, Wongmayura A, Nakabayashi M, et al. Boron cluster-based development of potent nonsecosteroidal vitamin D receptor ligands: direct observation of hydrophobic interaction between protein surface and carborane. J Am Chem Soc. 2011;133(51):20933-20941.

[11] Miljkovic D, Miljkovic N, McCarty MF. Up-regulatory impact of boron on vitamin D function—does it reflect inhibition of 24-hydroxylase? Med Hypotheses. 2004;63(6):1054-1056.

[12] Price CT, Langford JR, Liporace FA. Essential nutrients for bone health and a review of their availability in the average North American diet. Open Orthop J. 2012;6:143-149.

[13] Beattie JH, Peace HS. The influence of a low-boron diet and boron supplementation on bone, major mineral and sex steroid metabolism in postmenopausal women. Br J Nutr. 1993;69(3):871-884.

[14] Kidd PM. Vitamins D and K as pleiotropic nutrients: clinical importance to the skeletal and cardiovascular systems and preliminary evidence for synergy. Altern Med Rev. 2010;15(3):199-222.

[15] Rees K, Guraewal S, Wong YL, Majanbu DL, Mavrodaris A, Stranges S, et al. Is vitamin K consumption associated with cardio-metabolic disorders? A systematic review. Maturitas. 2010;67(2):121-128.

[16] Vassallo MF, Camargo CA Jr. Potential mechanisms for the hypothesized link between sunshine, vitamin D, and food allergy in children. J Allergy Clin Immunol. 2010;126(2):217-222.

[17] Hewison M, Zehnder D, Chakraverty R, Adams JS. Vitamin D and barrier function: a novel role for extra-renal 1 alpha-hydroxylase. Mol Cell Endocrinol. 2004;215(1-2):31-38.

[18] McElhanon BO, McCracken C, Karpen S, Sharp WG. Gastrointestinal symptoms in autism spectrum disorder: A meta-analysis. Pediatrics. 2014 Apr 28. [Epub ahead of print]

[19] de Magistris L, Familiari V, Pascotto A, Sapone A, Frolli A, Iardino P, et al. Alterations of the intestinal barrier in patients with autism spectrum disorders and in their first-degree relatives. J Pediatr Gastroenterol Nutr. 2010;51(4):418-424.

[20] Amminger GP, Berger GE, Schäfer MR, Klier C, Friedrich MH, Feucht M. Omega-3 fatty acids supplementation in children with autism: a double-blind randomized, placebo-controlled pilot study. Biol Psychiatry. 2007;61(4):551-553. Epub 2006 Aug 22.

Chapter Eleven
[1] Lerchbaum E, Obermayer-Pietsch B. Vitamin D and fertility: a systematic review. Eur J Endocrinol. 2012;166(5):765-778.

[2] Perrine CG, Sharma AJ, Jefferds ME, Serdula MK, Scanlon KS. Adherence to vitamin D recommendations among US infants. Pediatrics. 2010;125(4):627-632.

[3] Saad K, Cannell JJ, Bjørklund G, Abdel-Reheim MK. Vitamin D status in autism spectrum disorder and the efficacy of vitamin D supplementation in autistic children. Submitted for publication.

[4] Open-Label Clinical Trial of Vitamin D in Children with Autism. University of California, San Francisco. Clinicaltrials.gov. Available at: https://clinicaltrials.gov/ct2/show/NCT01535508?term=autism+and+vitamin+D&rank=2. Accessed July 2, 2014.

[5] Zerbo O, Iosif AM, Delwiche L, Walker C, Hertz-Picciotto I. Month of conception and risk of autism. Epidemiology. 2011;22(4):469-475.

[6] Hebert KJ, Miller LL, Joinson CJ. Association of autistic spectrum disorder with season of birth and conception in a UK cohort. Autism Res. 2010;3(4):185-190.

INDEX

Also Available from Sunrise River Press
Award-winning publisher of ground-breaking health, self-help & medical resources

THE ANTI-CANCER COOKBOOK
How to Cut Your Risk with the Most Powerful, Cancer-Fighting Foods

by Julia B. Greer, MD, MPH Dr. Julia Greer—a physician, cancer researcher, and food enthusiast—explains what cancer is and how antioxidants work to prevent pre-cancerous mutations in your body's cells and describes in detail which foods have been scientifically shown to help prevent which types of cancer. She shares her collection of more than 220 recipes loaded with nutritious ingredients and chock-full of powerful antioxidants that may significantly slash your risk of a broad range of cancer types, including lung, colon, breast, prostate, pancreatic, bladder, stomach, leukemia, and others. 7.5 x 9 inches, 224 pages. Softbound. *Item # SRP149*

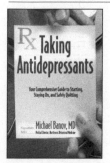

TAKING ANTIDEPRESSANTS
Your Comprehensive Guide to Starting, Staying On, and Safely Quitting

by Michael Banov, MD Antidepressants are the most commonly prescribed class of medications in this country. Yet, consumers have few available resources to educate them about starting and stopping antidepressants. Dr. Michael Banov walks the reader through a personalized process to help them make the right choice about starting antidepressants, staying on antidepressants, and stopping antidepressants. Readers will learn how antidepressant medications work, what they may experience while taking them, and will learn how to manage side effects or any residual or returning depression symptoms. Softbound, 6 x 9 inches, 304 pages. *Item # SRP606*

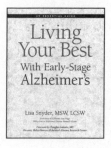

LIVING YOUR BEST WITH EARLY-STAGE ALZHEIMER'S
An Essential Guide

Lisa Snyder, MSW, LCSW Recent medical advances have made it possible to diagnose Alzheimer's when symptoms are only mild. Today, when a person is diagnosed they may have many years ahead with only mild symptoms. *Living Your Best with Early-Stage Alzheimer's: An Essential Guide* is a straightforward, practical guide on coping with the diagnosis, managing symptoms, finding meaningful activity, planning for the future, communicating, participating in research and clinical trials, and much more. This book helps the person with Alzheimer's feel empowered to move forward in life in light of this challenging diagnosis. 7 x 9 inches, 288 pages. Softbound. *Item # SRP603*

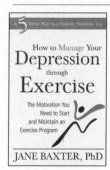

HOW TO MANAGE YOUR DEPRESSION THROUGH EXERCISE
The Motivation to Start and Maintain an Exercise Program

Jane Baxter, PhD Research has proven that exercise helps to lessen or even reverse symptoms of depression. Most depressed readers already know they need to exercise, but many can't muster the energy or motivation to take action. How to Manage Your Depression Through Exercise is the only book on the market that meets depressed readers where they are at emotionally, physically, and spiritually and takes them from the difficult first step of getting started toward a brighter future. Through the Move & Smile Five-Week Activity Plan, the Challenge & Correct Formula to end negative self-talk, and words of encouragement, author Jane Baxter uses facts, inspiration, compassion, and honesty to help readers get beyond feelings of inertia one step at a time. Includes reproducible charts, activities list, positive inner-dialogue comebacks, and photos illustrating various exercises. Softbound, 6 x 9 inches, 224 pages. *Item # SRP624*